Dear Kaye—
May this book
be a gift to you as it
has to me & may
your life itself continue
to be a gift. Love,
Martha

LIVING SIMPLY THROUGH THE DAY

Christmas
, 92

Living
Simply
Through
the Day
Spiritual Survival in a Complex Age

by
Tilden Edwards

PAULIST PRESS
New York, N.Y./Ramsey, N.J.

Library of Congress
Catalog Card Number: 77-14855

ISBN: 0-8091-2045-3

Published by Paulist Press
Editorial Office: 1865 Broadway, New York, N.Y. 10023
Business Office: 545 Island Road, Ramsey, N.J. 07446

Printed and bound in the
United States of America

Contents

ACKNOWLEDGMENTS

Science, theology, art, and personal experience all make clear our utter interdependence with all that is. Thus the thoughts of this book belong to me only as a personal screen for the countless people and forces that have poured through my life. A few of those people have been in the foreground of influence and helpfulness, and I want to recognize them here with my deep gratitude:

• My wife Ann for her soft, steady support and hard, discerning eye.

• Cecelia Braveboy and Devera Ehrenberg for their generous time in typing and critiquing the manuscript.

• Gerald May and Henry Atkins for their helpful suggestions.

• Lama Tarthang Tulku Rinpoché and Cistercian Abbot Thomas Keating for the fresh wisdom that led me deeper into Reality.

• The Steering Committee and people of the METC Shalem Institute for Spiritual Formation for their encouragement and many insights through the years.

• The Board of the Metropolitan Ecumenical Training Center for allowing me the time to write.

• El Retiro Jesuit Retreat House for the generous use of its facilities and fellowship for the most intensive period of writing.

• My two young children, Jeremy and Jennifer, for patiently leaving me alone to write in our basement for long hours.

• And, of course, my thanks at bottom to the Holy One, whose simple, subtle power and compassion always is being manifest among us.

I acknowledge with appreciation the permission of the National Council of Churches for the Biblical quotations from the Revised Standard Version of the Bible, copyrighted 1946, 1952, ©1971, 1973.

TO THE SIMPLE, HOLY HEART HIDDEN IN ALL OF US

Introduction

For my last birthday my wife gave me a ceramic sea otter to place on my desk. The otter is floating on its back, eating an abalone from a cracked shell: an alluring scene I have witnessed many times along the California coast.

To the casual eye that was a casual present. But it was far more. That otter is a reminder of much that I have come to appreciate about life in these last few years: the way we are held up when we attentively relax into it; the buoyancy this experience and trust gives us; the great energy available then to put into work and caring, yet work and caring that has a playful simple edge.

This sense of life is far from the heavy, grasping, tight, fearful orientation to life that dominated my earlier years— the churning attitude that muddies the water and sinks me into a murkiness of my own creation. Such heaviness, like a dark, obscuring rain cloud, can reappear out of the blue at any time and trap me. The otter sits on my desk as a reminder of the spacious, bright, confident, upholding, simple Presence that always is there, however obscured by passing clouds.

A cross sits on my desk, too. That sign has been near me all my life in this heavily churched land. Slowly, erratically, its significance has shifted from an opaque mass evoking a dull, listless response, to an oppressive sign of incomprehensible heaviness and torture, to an abstract symbol of abstract intellectual truths, to an open window into the way life is: broken and clouded, yet on its far side, whole and radiant.

Placing a cross and otter side by side as revealers of truth may seem absurd to some. But not to anyone who has experienced the cross as a sacrament, an opening into Reality's Heart. When we begin to see through the words and events of Jesus' life to their intimate yet infinitely vast Ground, then we begin to see through everything to that same Ground—even through otters! That Ground, which has a myriad of divine names born of human experience, unites and simplifies the day.

How I have begun to realize this truth in my own recent pilgrimage I would like to share with you first in this book. Then I will take you through certain basic windows of the day: waking, praying, relating, serving, eating, playing, aching, and sleeping. Each window is but a different facet of the same diamond through which we can see and participate in the uniting Ground, in the Holy One who shines through all.

We cannot control this "shining through" in us. That is a matter of grace, of gift. But we can learn to pay simple attention to what is happening; to be "recollected" in our deeper identity, rather than lost and scattered on the complex surface of the day. I have included many practical suggestions for cultivating this attentiveness in each daily activity.

Your participation in the simple, attentive way may be far more full than my own. I make no claim to spiritual maturity. The words I write are spoken at least as much to me as to you. Though these words will speak more often in trust and hope than personal realization, they are words that echo the experience of persons far more holy than I ever expect to be in this life. So perhaps the thoughts can be trusted beyond their speaker.

If I knew you personally, and you had come to me concerned with the simple way, I would choose some things for emphasis and demote, delete, or add others, according to your situation. Each of us is very unique, even though we share the same Ground. We each manifest that Ground differently. All of us need a very personal word: for us in this moment of our lives. I can only hope that somewhere in the chapters ahead the Spirit will rise, your situation and mine will touch, and the spark struck there will lighten your heart, clear your mind, and leave you a little more opened into the Holy One, in whom we live and move and have our being.

PART ONE: **Seeing Through Complexity**

Chapter One: A Personal Story

The Hands

An old German story[1] tells about the hands of God. God had never really finished making man, and thus had never seen a finished man. He determined to send His right hand into the world to take human form. That hand held all truth. But He was not fully satisfied with what He learned from this one hand. So He continues to send His left hand into the world. That hand is empty; it holds the space for search, for pilgrimage. Since man still is unfinished, goes the story, he must begin with the left hand. One cannot receive the fullness of the right hand except through the pilgrimage of the left.

As human beings our search is for the full truth of the right hand of God, which already is present. But our way to that fullness must be through a more and more empty left hand. A full left hand has no room to receive anything. It is cluttered and satiated and densely complex. As that hand empties, though, it becomes more and more simple and clear. The left hand then slowly unites with the right. We come ever closer to heeding Jesus' prescription for life: "Be perfect (allow your fulfillment) as your heavenly Father is perfect."

Fulfillment, perfection, is union of openness and fullness, two sides of one coin, one reality.

[1]Actually this is a composite of two German stories from Rilke and Lessing by the theologian John S. Dunne in *The Way of All the Earth* (Macmillan, 1972), pp. 93-95.

The Brain

A certain parallel to this story appears in modern brain research. The left side of our brain is the searching side: it grasps, manipulates, categorizes, makes time sequences. The right side of our brain, on the other hand, sees life whole. Everything is together, present, here now, intuitively known. There is no sense of linear time; no analysis. All is just given, full, complete. This right side seems to function best when the left side is quiet, open.

Recent Years

Only in the last few years have I begun to realize the great truth of this process of emptying to find, of simplifying in order to know what is most important. Most of my left hand pilgrimage has been made with the opposite assumption: fill yourself with everything possible; grasp for all you can; stuff your life with every thought, feeling, and experience available. The Kingdom will come at the top of that heap, when it is high and full enough.

But it does not come that way. What comes instead is a thicker pile of "stuff." As this clutter grows, the more fuel there is for the creation of yet more "stuff." And so the accumulation feeds upon itself. We find ourselves ever deeper into illusion, confusion, complexity. "And there is no health in us" (as the General Confession in the 1928 Book of Common Prayer acutely sums it up).

Turnaround

The great turnaround for me began four years ago. I had been working ecumenically in Washington, D.C. with the problems of clergy and congregations since 1967. My hope always was to help them accumulate the skills and knowledge they needed to be more effective in their ministries. I offered methods of planning and management, ways of working through differences within the congregation and developing a more open community, approaches to liturgical renewal, strategies for working with community issues of social justice, and many similar technologies and concerns. These indeed often did help people clarify their situations and work toward shared aims. But an underlying layer of truth rarely was touched. Subtle assumptions and motives concerning the nature of spiritual journey were not really exposed, challenged, or aided. At this ground level of perception out of which our actions flowed, it felt like the blind leading the blind.

In hindsight, I think most of us shared the illusion that the Kingdom did come through a stuffed left hand. There was a deep rumbling in myself and other people that was not being satisfied by such stuffing. Yet most of us had been raised in a church and society that believes stuffing is the way. So how else could we respond to the rumbling inside except by believing we needed yet more stuffing—more education, more activity, more people with us in church, more entertainment, more study, more accumulation of this or that? Our way of "helping" others usually assumed the same thing: others need more stuffing, too. A happy community is a stuffed one—bloated with everything possible.

Meditation

I had begun to taste guided silent meditation about this time through several weekend offerings. These included an introduction to certain Eastern as well as Western forms and approaches. Wanting something "more," I entered these experiences expecting to accumulate more "stuff." But that wasn't the way they turned out. For the first time, I was exposed to a way of letting go rather than taking on. Dim memories of times I had spent on retreat in monasteries came back to me. In those retreats there was no clear focus on the "self-clearing" forms of development that these new experiences centered upon. Yet the echo was there. Self-simplification, or "purgation" as we more ominously call it in Western spirituality, always was seen as crucial in Christian history, but its careful mental development has been sorely neglected. I began to see now that there was another way for the left hand that I had ignored. It could attentively open and let go, rather than grasp for more.

Sabbatical

Needing a deeper exposure to this dimly perceived way, I

arranged for a three month sabbatical from my work for the summer of 1973. I felt very open and vulnerable, knowing that I was moving into experientially unknown and vital territory. I didn't know where to go for further help. I didn't know whom to trust. Instinctively I felt the need for being with someone whose experience was very different from mine. Just about all the people I knew or knew of had come through the same basic American conditioning as I had concerning the left hand, where the job was to fill it up, not empty it. Turning to them would be turning to more of the same. Even if their subject was "emptying," I suspected they subtly would turn it into a way of possessing more.

California

When my sabbatical leave crept up on me in June I had made only one decision: I would go to California, that alluring symbol of the fresh start. Ten years of my life had been lived there, beginning at age twelve. That made it as close to home for me as anywhere, given the wanderings of my family as I grew up and my own voluntary moving around later. I have lived in every major section of the country at one time or another, but California, at least its northern coastal area, has retained a special radiance for me. The clear sun through the dry air, the cool breeze blowing off the Pacific, the semi-arid hills, the rolling fog that transforms the landscape endlessly, the meeting of Eastern and West-

ern cultures—all these invite the soul to see more clearly. Unfortunately, this potential usually is stillborn in the crush of ever more freeways, cars, industry, and people determined to possess all of this beauty and culture rather than allowing it to possess them—to grab these jewels as private objects rather than opening to their transforming power. Yet many try to be open. I wanted to go back and try to be open with them. I wanted to be in a physical-cultural environment that would coax my left hand to continue its unfreezing.

But where in particular to go? Whom to see? Being unsure that any satisfactory answer would come, I flew to San Francisco armed with dozens of books by spiritual masters. At least I could read alone on some hilltop, if nothing else more helpful appeared. That possibility faintly depressed me, though. Most great spiritual works are written for specific people in specific situations. The master sees the seeker's situation, then offers universal truth to him/her in the specific form that the person (or group or culture) can understand and live into it. I can piggy back on someone else's situation being addressed by a spiritual guide, but it rarely fits me exactly. I wanted to be with someone who could see and speak to me, uniquely, where I was. I wanted to give and take with that person, and be accountable with him/her for my responses over time.

Such desires frightened me. Allowing myself to be so vulnerable and susceptible with someone else risks being used, messed up, hurt. I had prided myself in the intellectual's independent, slightly skeptical attitude with others; maturity, I thought, meant keeping my ego in the driver's seat at all times, staying in control, striving for more knowledge (i.e., for more control). Even my years of therapy seemed to maintain this tacit assumption in its striving for more insight. And theology as well. Yet here I was feeling stifled and spiritually immature after thirty-seven years of life and eleven of priesthood. The only way out, the only way to real maturity now seemed to require letting go of what I had most prized, most developed, most relied upon: my firm, grasping left hand. Such irony!

John Weaver

After arriving in San Francisco I visited John Weaver, the Archdeacon of the Episcopal Diocese of California, on the advice of the Bishop of the Diocese, Kilmer Myers. John was a widely experienced priest with concerns and contacts in an amazing array of fields. I asked him, "Whom do you trust as a deeply developed Christian spiritual leader who can help me?"

His answer was similar to most other Church leaders I had spoken with: There was no one he unqualifiedly could recommend, especially not anyone proficient in the forms of meditation and experiential awareness that concerned me now. He echoed in his own way the chorus I had become familiar with, from cloistered religious and active Christians alike: the Church has not cultivated careful attentiveness to first hand, deeper spiritual awareness for a long time. We do have masters of concepts, and of community living, and of early stages of development, but extremely few who are masters of the progress of the soul in the way of a Teresa of Avila or John of the Cross.

John Weaver referred me to an unusual psychologist in Berkeley, Bill Soskin, who had sought out many spiritual leaders in the area over the years. John felt his wisdom could be trusted to know which if any appeared authentic and relevant to my situation.

Berkeley

In riding through Berkeley I was amazed to see what a transformation had taken place from its years as a citadel of mass political movements and leadership. Almost every lamp post now was plastered with posters advertising some way to spiritual well-being. Ads appeared for every variety of guru, bi-polar massage, primal scream therapy, spiritual communes, Jesus and Hasidic Jewish movements, forming a patchwork quilt that reflected the wide open, eclectic, indiscriminate search going on.

I felt sad that the political/social justice needs of life seemed cut off from the posters now. The ads seemed so private, so focused on the individual alone or in small groups. Yet here I was, too, searching, alone, for personal help—a kind of help neglected by the old Berkeley, and in its deeper stages by the Church, as well. In the rhythm of life and society this swing to personal search perhaps was inevitable. But in the back of my mind I felt uncomfortable. Distortion creeps into our vision and action when the 1960's social concern and the 1970's personal concern ignore each other. I yearned for a synthesis of these two, as two sides of one reality. Yet I knew this coalescence could not be forced. Right now an inner transformation was needed before I could bear ripe fruit in the social arena.

Bill Soskin

Bill Soskin impressed me as caring and in touch with his own and others' deeper spiritual needs. His approach with individual therapy clients could include nearly a whole day together, partly in silence, a far cry from the rigid fifty-minute, all-talk session of so many therapists. He also spent many hours weekly on a long-term project to provide special training for public school teachers that would better equip them to deal more deeply with the personal growth needs of students. He felt that such help ought not to be restricted to high-priced, private specialists, but should be instilled in the free public realm through a public servant position: the teacher. Here was an example of melding personal development and social concern that led me to a special respect for Bill. I also respected his willingness to integrate rational, emotional, and spiritual concerns as valid facets of one reality. He was a particularly "straight" intellectual researcher unabashedly mingling in a hip Berkeley world of emotional and spiritual quest. I felt his balance and caring. He could be trusted.

After telling him about my own background and quest, I asked my usual question,

"Whom can I turn to for help?"

This time I didn't restrict the possible source to a Christian.

Bill answered with a pointed question of his own:

"Are you really ready to roll up your sleeves and go to work, regardless of where it leads you, or do you just want to play games and not risk real change?"

I froze a little inside. Gnawing at the edge of my consciousness was the temptation to play the old game this summer, and accumulate a little more knowledge and pride. But a deeper voice inside said, "Yes, this is what you came for!"

Straightening up in my chair after a long pause, I finally said,

"Yes, I'm ready."

Next week, he said, one of the few authentic Eastern meditation/spiritual masters in this country, the Tibetan high lama Tarthang Tulku Rinpoché, would begin an intensive two-month program for people in the helping professions. For those who have less time, it could be entered for only two weeks.

Yes. It felt right—at least for two weeks. I didn't know if I wanted to put all my eggs in this one basket for the summer. It was a very unexpected and unknown and far-out basket, to say the least. Could I really trust it? There were other meditation/spiritual development programs in the area. Maybe after two weeks I should move on.

I thanked Bill for his help, and left feeling grateful for this new opportunity, whatever came of it. The next Monday I moved into the Nyingma Institute in Berkeley, the Tibetan study center of Tarthang Tulku Rinpoché.

Nyingma

The building is a huge ex-fraternity house on a hillside overlooking all of San Francisco Bay. It was painted in unique Tibetan colors and topped with flapping Tibetan prayer flags. As I looked up at this incredible sight I wondered what I was getting into! A flash of humiliation passed through me as I remembered my rather haughty Christian tradition. My search for spiritual help now threw me onto this strange shore which owed nothing to my tradition; in fact, the Tibetan tradition seemed the last intact major culture (until the recent Communist Chinese takeover) to owe nothing to Western civilization at all! I was in for a major cultural as well as spiritual challenge.

Before entering I offered a jumbled prayer that, in hindsight clarity, asked that I would stay open to the truth, stay in touch with the best of my own Western Christian roots, and be saved from getting lost in mere exotic trappings (and what could be more exotic than Tibet!). I came seeking ways of purging the clutter of my life. If I wasn't careful, I saw that moving into such a radically different milieu could add more clutter, and confusion to boot. But here I was, and here I intended to stay—at least for two weeks!

Walking up the steep hill and long staircase to the main entrance was like a small pilgrimage in itself. At the top I was greeted by a great pile of shoes. Adding mine to it, I entered that much lighter, quieter, cleaner, and more naked. I remember Moses' experience with God in the burning bush when he was instructed to take off his shoes, "for the place on which you are standing is holy ground" (Ex. 3:5). The commonality of this practice in other great religious traditions came to mind as well. The only Christian place I have come across in the West that practices naked feet in the temple is the Spiritual Life Institute in Sedona, Arizona. It felt right there. It felt right here.[2]

Most of the fifty-odd participants in the program turned out to be therapists, with a scattering of teachers, artists, and others. I was the only priest. In fact, I was one of only a few persons who was active in any Western religious path,

[2]"The shoes we take off are made from the skin of dead animals. As long as we wear them, there is something dead between the live soles of our feet and the ground on which we are standing. To take off this deadness means taking off the familiarity which breeds contempt and boredom: it means coming alive in

though all participants were Westerners. Being used to a Church milieu, with all the tacit assumptions that go with that shared commitment, I now found myself just another private seeker among others. The one commitment held in common was to spend time with Rinpoché (a title by which the lama was called by everyone). There was no inclusive commitment to one another—even to learn each other's names. Rinpoché did have a monastery with about one hundred members a mile away. That involved much more extensive commitments. The Nyingma Institute, on the other hand, is a "secular" study center, for those who do not plan to undertake full commitment to the Buddhist Way.

This lack of a shared deep commitment together both relieved and plagued me all summer. I felt relief in being an anonymous person who could come and go as I pleased, do the work assigned by Rinpoché if I felt like it, speak to or ignore others, take it all seriously or play with it around the fringes. This comfortable looseness reinforced by others had a price, though: there was no mutual reinforcement or security for really letting go, for allowing the hard work of opening, emptying, and giving myself over to happen.

I became vividly aware of the impact of community on where and how far one usually goes in personal development. Looking back through religious history I saw why there has been such emphasis on careful forms of shared discipline and commitment. And why so many great saints

primordial freshness to the place where we are" (David Steindl-Rast, O.S.B., "The Environment as Guru", *Cross Currents*, special issue: "Word Out of Silence," Vol. 24, nos. 2-3, p. 151).

were moved to leave human community altogether for a few months or years when it became an inadequate stimulus for transformation.

Rinpoché

The one great stimulus for all of us that summer was Rinpoché himself. His background, bearing, intelligence, energy, and warmth combined to make him a powerful magnet for those seeking a guide into deeper reaches of reality.

Born into a lama's family in Eastern Tibet, he was "discovered" as a child to be a reincarnate high lama, a "tulku," and as such was given twenty years of the most strict and careful education with the best gurus available. That education wove together art, psychology, meditation, devotional practices, philosophy, and forms of physical relaxation and healing, into a single reinforced fabric of awareness. The great weight fell on the development of first-hand experience—first hand awareness—that cut through layers of illusion, fear, and desire. Such development included many months alone in caves, paying attention to his mind, learning to see and reduce its scatteredness and grasping, to literally realize its basic nature, and to cultivate a deep compassion for all sentient beings. Such discipline led to certain psychic powers, which in his tradition always are considered by-products not to be focused upon, lest they become ego power trips.

Rinpoché never would speak of or even admit to these powers. Yet many persons present had clear evidence of his knowing things about them (including things that had not yet happened) that he could not have known without the capacity to be in their minds, and the capacity for a timeless dimension of perception. This is not to say that he was "all-knowing"; he was subject to the limitations and failings of all mortals. Yet his gifts of perception clearly were developed beyond those of us sitting before him that summer.

Needless to say, such unspoken powers created an extra aura of mystery and fascination around him. That Rinpoché did not exploit this fascination led me to trust him more. In fact, he projected a very everyday personality, marked especially by an earthy humor and personal warmth and concern. He never tried to sound dramatic or awesome. He always seemed to accept you where you were, to speak on your level, to mirror your situation, to be "with you" in a way that helped you relax and loosen up. At the same time, there always was a subtle challenge to let go of your own laziness, selfishness, lack of confidence, complacency, or egotistical seriousness, whichever he perceived was blocking you. In fact, his ultimate challenge was to let go of everything. "Nothing holding anything anywhere," in mind or body—that was his repeated theme. Everything he taught was a means to that end: a great range of meditation forms, psychological and physical methods for lightening emotional attachments, philosophical concepts, disciplines for daily living, all aimed at a kind of pure iconoclasm that left nothing to cling to: an empty left hand that indeed was free to receive from the fullness of truth in the right hand.

West Meets East

After an average day of twelve hours of meditation (together and alone), lecture, and dialogue, including three silent, vegetarian meals, I saved just enough energy to open the Gospels and read for a while each day. Part of this was a defensive reaction: I didn't want to lose my own spiritual lineage. Part of my motivation was open concern: I wanted to see what would happen in a daily dialogue between Jesus and Gautama, between the Christ and the Buddha. Would they deeply clash or coincide? So many books had been written about their relation, with as many contradictory conclusions.

I was amazed to find how many of the difficult sayings of Jesus began to appear freshly lucid—what it means to "lose your life to find it," for Jesus to be "in the Father and we in Him and He in us," for a sound eye to lead the whole body to be full of light, for the Kingdom to be in our midst, and on and on.

So much of my biblical education had been focused on analysis and interpretation of the text. Now the words were clicking intuitively in relation to my developing first-hand attentiveness and letting go in meditation and daily living.

An inkling of Jesus' possible awareness behind His words began to trickle into my consciousness. I felt a new intimacy and closeness with Him. Indeed, I began to feel a depth of trust in Him that I had never known.

Seeing the intuitive powers of Rinpoché at work brought me even closer. I sensed a little what it must have been like to be around someone like Jesus who had the capacity to see through you and show compassion for what He saw. In the light of the many miracles of healing and other powers in Tibetan tradition, I also began to accept more readily Jesus' miraculous powers. Nothing any longer needed to be de-mythologized. Everything was possible. Walking on water, resurrection. Why not? The divine image in man uniquely manifest in Jesus[3] provides enormous potential for human sight and action. Though this image is obscured in our own tragic, willful blindness, yet it is there with us: the right hand of God always ready to be received. The words of a contemporary Roman Catholic theologian, John Dunne, came sharply home to me:

> What seems to be occurring is a phenomenon we might call "passing over," passing over from one culture to another, from one way of life to another, from one religion to another. Passing over is a shifting of standpoint, a going over to the standpoint of another culture . . . way of life . . . religion. It is followed by an equal

[3]*Unique* manifestation here does not mean an *exclusive* one. In the theologian Raimundo Pannikar's words: "These revelations (of the great world religions) do not equate; they are unique, they're not contradictory. It's a very simple thing" (*Cross Currents*, op. cit.).

*and opposite process we might call "coming back,"
coming back with new insight to one's own culture . . .
way of life . . . religion. . . . Passing over and coming
back, it seems, is the spiritual adventure of our time.*[4]

Gospels and Experience

This isn't to say that everything jelled perfectly between
the Gospels and my new daily experience. But much more
was radiant, alive, and together than ever before.

This became most clear one Sunday morning when I participated in the Solemn Eucharist at Grace Cathedral atop
Nob Hill in San Francisco. I had spent three hours in a form
of meditation taught by Rinpoché before going. I walked in
and sat in the middle of everyone. My mind was quiet and
open. The celebrants moved and spoke and broke bread
with an even, rhythmic dignity that concretely continued my
meditation, revealing life together through and beyond the
liturgical words and actions.

Looking around me I was startled to sense the boredom,
restlessness, and fidgeting of others. How many times I had
felt that way! But now it amazed me—how could anyone not
be caught up in this awesome dance of reconciled life? This
exposure of the very nature of reality, of God and man and
nature, known and unknown? Never again would I forget
the importance of preparation for Eucharist. Without it,
liturgy so easily becomes complicated form without sub-

[4]John S. Dunne, *The Way of All the Earth* (Macmillan, 1972), p. ix.

stance, truth hidden by a distracted "mosquito mind" (to borrow a phrase of an early Church Father).

Simply There

I did not leave after two weeks. To go to bits and pieces of retreats and talks in other centers now would be like bobbing up and down on the surface for the rest of the summer. I felt myself being pulled down from a cluttered, unaware, driven surface consciousness to a place of calm clarity and unattached (not *de*-tached) caring. The surface was still there with all of its desires and fears, yet it was a bit lighter, more relativized, less important, just "there." My usually hard surface of identity was becoming a permeable mesh through which a deeper, truer Self could be freed and given room for effect.

Endless words have been given to this Self, with soul or divine image being most familiar to us. Desiring not to reduce it to less than it is, Buddhists tend to describe it negatively or cryptically in such phrases as "no-mind". Christian mystics in their own way have done the same. All words are inadequate. Perhaps the only important thing to say is that this reality belongs to all of us, indeed, *is* us when we are most clear. It is our bridge to God, to the Heart of Reality; it is our open window, and thus not really an "it" at all, but that which is there before any "it" appears, and after every "it" dissolves: the simple "thereness" that seamlessly unites all.

Final Interview

At the end of the two months I had a long private interview with Rinpoché, my third of the summer. No two months of my life had ever been so full, at a time when I was so ready to learn (and unlearn!). An immense horizon was opened to me which was much too vast and bright to more than glimpse in so short a time. No religious boundary lines made sense at this point—the truth felt too big for that. And yet Rinpoché had reinforced and respected my own Christian particularity throughout the summer; he insisted that one needs to go down deeply into one "lineage," one deep tradition.

He had meant so much to me at that point that I asked if I could be his Christian "chela," his student. He laughed and said our karma had brough us together, and this was a gift.

"I am your Tibetan priest-friend, Tilden. We are priest brothers. You don't need to be a Buddhist student. You can learn everything I have to offer and use it within your own Tradition. There is nothing to gain by crossing over. It is all there available as a Christian."

This non-proselytizing response increased my respect for him, though I felt a little cheated. There was so much more I needed to let go, and to learn. He helped me realize, though, that this "work" can go on all the time, at any place. No master and no tradition can do your work for you. I must allow myself to let go of endless obscuring attachments still with me and see the Kingdom in the midst of daily life—and pray for the grace that lets this surrendering and seeing happen. There is no place to go but here and now. Here and now is your teacher, if you allow it to be. Every here and now can be useful.

The interview ended sitting on the floor together, face to face, eye to eye. Rinpoché asked me to think of the people and places I was returning to. As I did this, his eyes seemed to disappear deep inside me, as though he were transmitting himself into my future life. When he "came back" to everyday consciousness, he asked me, "What happened to your mind?" After my fumbling response, he casually ignored the whole episode, softly spoke of our families and future meeting again, and wished me well.

Christian Retreat

Before returning home I wanted to spend a transitional week in an intensive Christian setting. I needed more time to integrate my experience with some classical Christian ways before jumping back into my educational work with clergy and laity. An eight-day Jesuit Ignatian retreat felt as though it would be just right, given its daily rhythm of scriptural meditation, personal reflection, spiritual direction, and Eucharist.

I arranged for this at the Wernersville, Pennsylvania Jesuit

Center for Spiritual Growth. One of the most revealing experiences of that week was time spent reading (or rereading) from some of the great Christian contemplatives: Ruysbroeck, Tauler, John of the Cross, Teresa of Avila, Thomas Merton and others. I nearly leapt from my chair when some passages seemed to describe the same awareness of reality that Rinpoché had asserted during the summer. It became clear to me that the same profound pristine awareness is shared by many Eastern and Western masters, but this preverbal awareness, once translated into pictorial and verbal consciousness by our minds, breaks into a myriad of interpretations conditioned by the symbols and experiences of our particular culture. The shared original awareness is the immensely spacious, compassionate, imageless image of God shining through us, revealing an indestructible unity through endlessly changing forms.

The Return

I returned from that summer feeling like someone returning from another planet. Could my experience possibly make sense to the people I work with? Could Rinpoché's approach to seeing and dealing with reality be enriching for them, or more confusing, complicating, and threatening?

Soon after returning I began work with a group of clergy, religious and laity committed to explore self-clearing, self-simplifying forms of meditation and spiritual development weekly together for eight months. I received their permission to work almost exclusively for the first four months with Tibetan Buddhist approaches to relaxing, stilling, and clearing the body and mind. Behind this request was my new sense of the value of stepping outside the familiar forms of our own tradition for a while into those of another more actively intuitive, contemplative tradition, and then circling back to our own with fresh eyes.

"Mystical" perhaps would be a better term here than contemplative, in Evelyn Underhill's sense of the art of union with Reality. But the connotations of mystical in our society are so frequently distorted that I have felt it best to choose a more open word: "contemplative." Contemplation more narrowly refers to a specific stage of spiritual awareness beyond controlled stages of meditation, marked by a given (not willed) abandonment. My use of it will be more broad, referring to the art of union with the Real, through the path of development that values inner solitude in the midst of caring community: space for energetic, attentive, ever-simplifying, lightening awareness.

This path also is kin to what is called "apophatic" in Western religious history: a way of understanding God, as Francis Martin puts it, where "formulations are the sides of a dyke, and the truth is the beautiful clear water in the middle" (*Cross Currents*, op. cit., p. 258). Evagruis Ponticus, an early Church Father, stands in this way when he says:

"Blessed are those who have reached *infinite* ignorance" (*Ibid.*, p. 169).

Such is the way of full simplicity.

In East Indian tradition, this path is akin to "jnana yoga," that path of intuitive wisdom which "aims directly at the 'mystery,' " which "does not allow the mind to get dispersed in . . . imagination or abstract thought," a state which is "an awakening, of which nothing can be said except 'Asa,' 'that is that.' " . . . It is "total simplicity, pure transparency" (a description by the Benedictine monk H. Le Saux [Abhishiktananda], "Experience of God in Eastern Religions, *Cistercian Studies*, Vol. IX, 1974, pp. 32-33).

I was greatly relieved to find that what was true for me proved true for most of those clergy and laity. Rather than alien and strange, the Tibetan practices we used for some actually led to a more intimate sense of home. Together we saw how neglected the contemplative strain of Christian tradition was in our conditioning, and how much it could illumine our understanding and actions. It felt as though God's aim of reconciliation on this planet now pressed proud Christians finally to appreciate Eastern religious experience as a way of rediscovering certain depths of our own tradition. Easterners in turn have been pressed to rediscover the positive social/political implications of their own religious ways through experience with Judaeo-Christian historical/social concerns.

Shalem

Hundreds of clergy, religious, and laity have joined such spiritual development groups since that first one. In 1975 a new Institute for Spiritual Formation was created to provide a coherent base for further exploration and development. The Institute has another name, "Shalem," a Hebrew word meaning "to be complete, whole." It is a component of the Metropolitan Ecumenical Training Center of Washington, D.C. Besides its focus on contemplative spirituality, Shalem is concerned with exploring fresh ways of integrating social action and contemplation, psychology and spiritual development, maleness and femaleness, as these relate to the spiritual journey.

The value of long-term, disciplined mutual exploration has been so important for some individuals that they have never stopped. Many of those in the original group still meet weekly, for the fifth year now. One perceptive member aptly described the groups as analagous to a medieval pilgrimage: people join when they're ready and leave when they're ready; a great variety of people come together; it is an intensive, open period of time; and no established religious institutions are replaced—rather, the pilgrimage indirectly enriches those bodies.

World Story

As I read human history now, I see that what has happened with us is but a continuation of a very long pilgrimage, a common story that begins symbolically with Abraham's call to leave the familiarity and security of his home to wander in naked faith toward the Promised Land. Trusting and seeing through the events of his life to its Ground became the steady thread of his life.

That call to naked faith is in us all. For me it appears full-blown in my spiritual father, Jesus Christ. Its radiance illumines the Prophets, the Psalmists, St. Paul, the Desert Fathers and Mothers, the deep spiritual lineages of many peoples. In America it reaches simple purity in that Shaker lyric now embedded in our religious folk music:

It's a gift to be simple
It's a gift to be free
It's a gift to come down
Where you ought to be
And when you see yourself in a way that is right
You will live in a valley of love and delight!

Naked faith at its fullest is simplicity itself, an orientation that unburdens God of every false accretion. Followers of Muhammed express this when they proclaim "There is no God but God"—a powerful summary of the First Commandment: "You shall have no other gods besides me."

A Zen master puts it in a fresh way:

There is no God!
But He's always with you.[5]

[5]Joshu Sasaki Roshi, *Buddha Is the Center of Gravity* (Lama Foundation, San Cristobal, New Mexico), 1974, p. 12

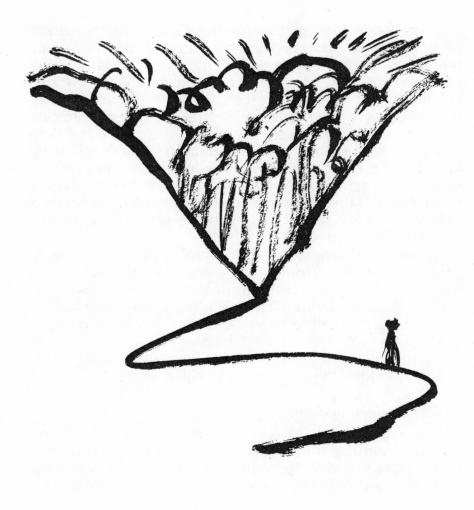

As the years pass by, I increasingly appreciate the great weight spiritual masters place on everyday, plain living as the path of naked, simple faith.[6] Once the fascination with new ways recedes, once you become clear that loving and enlightenment cannot be forced, then the primary attitude that emerges is patient, attentive trust. There is enormous value in Eastern and Western spiritual disciplines, but they guarantee nothing. Their value is greatest when they help us lighten our greedy, self-serious striving—when they free us to be self-forgetfully, gently, simply present, here and now, in the midst of the dishes, an aching back, a history book, a fight, office work, a kiss, waiting for the plane, a meeting to plan action against some social ill.

Spiritual development is not complicated, but it is very subtle. Its "work" is primarily "undeveloping" our conditioning to grasp, possess, get, judge, and keep—opening the clinging, bloated left hand. The more that hand opens, the more it is possible to see and receive what already is present, the right hand of God, heaven in our midst. Words and concepts can't grasp this presence. But simple attentiveness, moment by moment, can open us for it.

Simply Undevelopment

That word "simple" has struck me lately as the unifying thread of spiritual life, that is, of life at its fullest and most real. Before we "do" something to life with our complicating fears and desires, it is simple, just there, radiant, to-

---

[6]Listen, for example, to Thomas Merton: "In practice the way to contemplation is an obscurity so obscure that it is no longer even dramatic. There is nothing left in it that can be grasped and cherished as heroic or even unusual. And so, for a contemplative there is a supreme value in the ordinary routine of work and

gether, flowing, in God. We always have the choice of seeing reality as it is and being with it, or seeing reality as our fears and desires warp it. When we know this choice exists, then our real freedom is born. Then even when we act out of some cloudy craziness, there will be a still, small voice that gently laughs and knows that this moment can obscure only temporarily the radiant simplicity of God in our midst.

Living Simply

Living in our externally complex, wavering, careening, fragmented culture, we easily lose sight of the simple thread of grace[7] uniting all. Then we readily add to the culture's murkiness. In the chapters ahead I will share with you some little ways that can help us to be attentive, simply present in daily living. You may be tempted to use these ways as techniques to force rather than allow God's hand, or to incorporate them indiscrimately in your life as a protective patched quilt. These temptations are in us all. The writer of Ecclesiastes saw this temptation when he said: "God made man upright, but they have sought out many devices" (Eccl. 7:29). The suggestions I offer are not new "devices" that take us further away from our uprightness. They are means of seeing and shedding our devices so that our natural uprightness can emerge.

They are not magical, blanket prescriptions for everyone,

---

poverty and hardship and monotony that characterize the lives of all the poor and uninteresting and forgotten people in the world" (from *Seeds of Contemplation*).

[7]Grace at its simplest expresses the way life happens in faith: as open, free gift, through and beyond and despite all we do.

but stimulants that can help evoke your own unique calling day by day, your own organic pattern of awakening, your own strength to stand nakedly in the Holy Presence.

Just as we cannot evade our unique journey, neither can we evade the enormous complexities woven into our society and personal lives, but perhaps we can be less lost in them, and thus able to contribute more penetrating light than cloudy heat. Then we might realize what it means to be in the world, but not of it.

Both Eastern and Western sources inspire these suggestions for simple living through the day. If you already are committed to exploring and participating in the Truth within a particular deep spiritual tradition, these different sources can be enriching.[8] If you find yourself "floating" now, committed through no particular tradition, then I hope these offerings from different sources will not keep you floating, but will press you toward commitment and community within one deep lineage.

We may not be able to commit ourselves wholeheartedly at the moment to a particular institutional expression of a deep tradition, due to our own past scars and stillbirths within these frail vessels. But at least we can commit ourselves to the enlightened awareness, the Revelation, in the tradition itself, which is far more than any one particular institutional expression of it. Whenever possible, we need

---

[8]It can be a relief for some to note here that a living tradition is not rigid, static something we stand under. It is a particular tide of deep human/divine experience and awareness that continues to flow through us. We each live in that tide

to claim the institution for the real depth of its tradition, working mightily to allow the river of grace to flow freely through it, minimally blocked by individual and collective empire building, exploitation, and confused ignorance (especially our own!).

If we do not allow ourselves to go down deeply somewhere, we are in danger of floating on the surface in an erratic, eclectic, unaccountable, and lonely way. Our humanity calls for particularity—a particular channel of grace.

My own primary channel through Jesus Christ, and the historical and living community that takes seriously His claimed intimacy with ultimate Truth, offers a very personal, particular "way in" to universal reality. My commitment to Truth through Him opens my eyes to grace everywhere. He is not someone to protect and defend. He reveals the Loving Light that frees me to live in the naked simplicity of *nothing* ultimately to protect and defend. Then I am free to claim every moment and person as friend—and to see the grace in every tradition as mine; as part of our common human treasure.

If the effect of commitment is the opposite—a closing off, cornering, and boxing of the truth in a sectarian and imperious way—that to me is sacrilege. If you refuse to identify with that way in its various institutional expressions, then I firmly join hands with you. Authentic commitment opens rather than closes. It is commitment to embrace the truth,

in a unique, exploratory way. Such attentive living is our spirituality, our "experiment in continuity" (to borrow Martin Thornton's phrase in *English Spirituality*, S.P.C.K., London).

wherever it is, whatever its form, but in recognition that our "way in" to the truth must be some deep way in particular. That way can lead us everywhere that truth lives.

All truth is in one rarefied yet earthly room, but our awareness often is outside. We need to open a particular door and go through its conditioning chamber, gradually preparing ourselves to be able to see and respond in the subtle, awesome, caressing light of that spacious room. Different conditioning chambers, different traditions, can offer each other a great deal of help out of their different experiences. This help is particularly available and important to receive today. Such sharing can improve the catholicity—the fullness—of a particular chamber. Still, through one chamber most of us need to pass for full conditioning.[9]

[9]"All ways may lead to Rome, but this statement entails two conditions: that we march on those ways, without stopping short of the end—i.e., that the ways be really ways—and that we do not jump transversally from one way to another, but follow one particular way with patience and the hope that we shall meet at least at the end of our journey if our ways do not cross earlier . . . We should be aware of the danger of shallowness inherent in any search for universality": Raimundo Panikkar, "Non-Dualistic Polarities," Cross Currents, Vol. 24, nos. 2-3, p. 154. "Trees which are repeatedly transplanted do not grow roots": St. Gregory of Sinai.

PART TWO: **Simple Presence Through The Day**

Chapter Two: Grounding

Grounding

It is late evening. We are alone, perhaps for the first time since we awoke. Bits and pieces from the day dart in and out of our consciousness. Little desires and fears for tomorrow scatter us further. The more that rushes through our minds, the more complicated and anxious life seems. Maybe TV will help settle us down—or the newspaper—or some work—or sex—or a big snack. Less seems to gnaw at us then. Life stays put for a moment. We feel in control again—we're "doing" something—anything.

The after-effect of the doing leaves us less anxious, but more drugged. We've exchanged a gnawing anxiety for a dulled sensibility. Maybe, at least, we can sleep now. We do, on the surface. But not below. Our dreams are troubled. Fragments of life whir round and round without a center. We wake tired, and struggle out for another round.

> Has not man a hard service upon earth,
>   and are not his days like the days of a hireling?
> Like a slave who longs for the shadow,
>   and like a hireling who looks for his wages,
> So I am allotted months of emptiness
>   and nights of misery are apportioned to me.
>
> When I lie down I say, "When shall I arise?"
>   But the night is long,
>   and I am full of tossing till the dawn. (Job 7:1-4)

You and I share such an "underlife." It usually is bearable; it even seems "normal," out of sheer habit. Sometimes it is even fun. But it is not fulfilling. We are grown for more than that. When this becomes most clear, when the whole daily round feels most wearisome, we hear ourselves crying out in the Psalmist's lament:

How long, O Lord? Will you forget me forever?
How long will you hide your face from me? (Ps. 13:1)

How long must I tromp through this dense jungle half crazed and blind before the clearing appears?

If the energy of our anger and desperation runs deep and long, then perhaps we are ready to let the clearing appear. The amazing thing is that the clearing always is present right where we are. Usually it is hidden beneath a great, dense pile of "stuff": scattered thoughts, driving feelings, jerky body, crowded environment. When in our anger and desperation this clutter catches fire and begins to lighten, we might be gifted with fresh sight. Suddenly we "see through" the clutter, if only for an instant. What we see then is transparent and luminous, light and spacious, warm and full, a great dance united at every point. For a flash we are fully present in a simple whole.

Such wondrous opening we could call the Holy Spirit's

transforming window. When it is open, the moment is open for insight and warmth, for wisdom and compassion.

How can we live out of the simple, holy spaciousness that is there always in our midst? That is in and through everything that is? How can we allow simple purity of heart, so we with Jesus can see life in God, instead of seeing it just neck deep in clutter?

Anger and desperation may start us off. But we need far more if the clearing we have glimpsed in fact or hope is not quickly to be lost sight of again.

There is no grand, clear-cut path. But there are many little ways we can simplify our inner life during the day. These ways can rake the leaves of our flighty, cluttered lives to the outer ring of consciousness. The center can be left simple, open, spacious. Of course, the leaves blow back over the center with every gust of wind. And there are so many layers of leaves! Raking must be constant and long.

Firm commitment, deep acceptance, and naked confidence are three vital prerequisites of the simple way. Each of these attitudes has endlessly subtle layers of awareness. At the bottom of each lies the divine image in us, reflecting the very nature of God.

We need a clear *commitment* to holy simplicity. Without it, we will not have the energy and attentiveness to "see through" our fascinations with all the leafy clutter. As I once heard Ram Dass[10] say, we must really *want* God, which is far

---

[10]Baba Ram Dass, the ex-Harvard psychologist Richard Alpert turned Guru. His book *Remember, Be Here Now* has many helpful suggestions for simple, holy living.

more (and far simpler) than merely wanting to want God.

We need a deep *acceptance* of ourselves—of all that is there, known and unknown. Even acceptance of our non acceptance. Total acceptance. Without full acceptance, we will distort the way of simplicity into a way of avoiding what we most fear or hate in ourselves. Or we will seek to root out sin and illusion with violence rather than compassion.

Above all, we need to enter each day with a naked *confidence*. God will not give us more than we can bear. God is Loving Mystery beyond our understanding, beyond our atheism or theism or agnosticism. There is grace in all things. The very nature of life is confident. So you can afford to relax into the day, without controlling expectations. Without this naked confidence, we will use the way of simplicity to secure and not free us, to create a protected other world rather than a fresh embrace with one indivisible world.

Since these three attitudes are so important to the simple way, they need very special attention. They are incomplete in all of us. Their growth is a gift beyond our full command. So before reading further, let me urge you to put the book down a moment. Close your eyes. Gently see yourself in the light of these needs. Then offer a fervent prayer that each basic attitude may be uncovered in you ever more fully.

Practicing the little ways of simplification suggested in the pages ahead can encourage these three gifts. They are the ground that must always be remembered and nurtured.

Chapter Three: The Simple Day

Retreat

Nearly twenty years ago I spent three days at Holy Cross Monastery, an Episcopal religious community on the Hudson River that maintains ordered, classical monastic daily life. That was my first experience in a monastery. I didn't talk much with the brothers. I just shared their daily rhythm of life and let its impact take its course.

The impact was powerful. Gradually shedding the striving, fearful, anxious, "crowded" consciousness that I brought with me, I knew more moments of "simple presence" than I had ever known.

One Gift

Why did this happen? It has not always happened that way in monastic retreats since then, so first of all I'm clear that the experience involves a gift that the community couldn't guarantee. But I know its daily "way" encouraged the gift. That way as I see it hallows a balanced rhythm of human activity: working, corporate worship, individual study and prayer, recreation, eating, sleeping; time alone and time together; time to be silent and time to speak; a time and place for everything. These are not seen as unconnected fragments of a day, though; they are different aspects of a single reality; different doors for the same divine energy; different opportunities for realizing simple presence. They are connected by the single thread of grace out of which everything flows.

No part of the day then is more "special" than any other

part. No activity is more holy than any other. There is nothing anxiously to look forward to, and nothing ultimately to fear. The whole day is a varied screen through which the same Light filters. Such awareness enormously simplifies the day.

Social Contrast

The simple day stands in stark contrast to the major press of our society. Balance is not supported. "Settling" time particularly is neglected: time to be still alone and together, time to simply "be." There is a crazy oscillation between mindless work and mindless play, between one driving impulse and another. The day is a kaleidoscope of bits and pieces connected by nothing, expressing no real common ground. The result is a kind of personal and societal fragmentation, a desperate and futile effort to hold it all together, a pathless, complex jungle that leaves so many people insecure, angry, frightened, confused, and easy prey for the first simplistic savior that comes along.

Yet we must find our way in the midst of this society that in the main does not support or understand simplicity. To the degree that the Church loses itself in our society's confusions, it loses its own way and cannot help us either. But simplicity always is there. It cannot be lost, only hidden. In the cracks of our cultural fabric today its presence and importance creeps through.

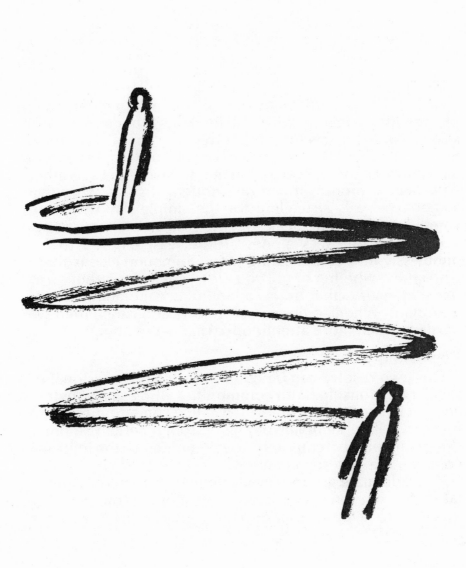

Friends

Unless we are particularly heroic or saintly persons, each of us needs a relationship with at least one other person who also seeks and trusts the simple way, the Simple Presence. Such a "spiritual friend" can be enormously supportive to us, and we to them. Even if you meet or write to each other only once a month, it can be enough. Just knowing that someone else is struggling for the simple day with you, whether or not you speak together often, is encouraging. You feel a little less alone, a little less tempted to fall mindlessly into complicating traps. Someone else is there who knows whether or not you are trying to pay attention to the simple way; that brings a kind of accountability that is important. When someone else knows and cares, then we pay that much more attention to what we're doing.[11]

Community

Our own resolve can be enhanced also by occasional or regular relationships with communities whose daily rhythm and intent support the simple day. Such communities range from formal contemplative ones, through certain summer camps and other "temporary" communities, to the informal common life of certain families.

If no adequate group is available to you, then don't hesitate to feel out some friends about developing your own way together, for a few days or on a more long-term basis. There

[11]The courageous Vietnamese monk, Thich Nhat Hanh, so important to the humanity of Vietnam during its inhuman war, says this in speaking of going through the crises that are inevitable for a person "who lives his religion": "The friend is at your side, even if he does nothing for you during this period of crisis,

are many people around you who hunger for such an opportunity. Remember, we are talking about a need for simplicity that is natural, that belongs to all. Not everyone, of course, is ready to move at the same time or in the same way. Those closest to us in other ways may be far from us at the moment in this opening to simplicity. But a few people always are near who are ready in the way you are. It may take some time to find them, but if you keep your eyes open, you will.

There is an old Eastern saying: "The guru appears when you are ready for him." We could shift that slightly and say: "The spiritual friend or community we need appears when we are ready for them."[12]

Interior Life

Developing such an environment of support is very important. But we must be clear that it is not sufficient. We cannot look to community or a balanced rhythm in the day to save us. We indeed are "saved" in community, and for community, but not by it. No environment or other person can do more than encourage our interior simplicity. That comes by personal attentiveness and grace, from the moment we awake through our dreams in the night.

even if he says nothing to comfort you. The way he looks at you is something you need. There was one time when I underwent a crisis, and with me there was only a cat to look at me; and that helped a lot" (*The Raft Is Not the Shore*, Daniel Berrigan and Thich Nhat Hanh, Beacon, 1975, p. 136).

[12]I have mentioned spiritual friend rather than spiritual director (or father or mother) for two reasons. The first is because a good director *is* a spiritual friend, standing strongly *beside* us in our opening to God. The second reason is that

Chapter Four: Waking
Opening The Day

Simple Seeing

Emerging from that twilight between sleep and waking, we notice our drowsiness, the light, the pillow, the room. Quickly we leap from this simple seeing to something more: the drowsiness turns to memory of a late night, the light to awareness of a rainy day, and trying to remember where we left our umbrella. The pillow case is dingy: when did we change the bedding last? The room clicks off snatches of other random thoughts and feelings.

Within seconds of waking, our minds are off and running: scattered and judging. The growing whirl clouds and complicates our sight like a swirl of leaves in an autumn gust. What can we do?

First notice what is happening without judgment. See the leaves whirling around. Smile gently into yourself. Simplify that scattered energy by going backward: the room, the pillow, the light, the drowsiness. They just are. Let them be there a few seconds, without doing anything to them. Then let that energy focus wordlessly on your abiding intention for confidence, acceptance, and simplicity.

Simple Praying

If active prayer during the day is your custom, let it first come now. Keep it simple: a simply felt solidarity with suffering and grace. End by turning the day over, letting it be,

---

advanced spiritual guides, fully worthy of the title "director," are very sparse among us. Listen to these rare gifts needed by a full-blown spiritual guide as described by Kallistos Ware ("The Spiritual Father in Orthodox Christianity," "relaxing into God." Let the last seconds before rising be very still, clear, calm—just be there. Young children bursting into the room and other kinds of "fast starts" don't always allow such a beginning. Sometimes this all must be telescoped into a few seconds. But at least assure yourself those.

Simple Activity

Now slowly rise. Don't jerk yourself out of bed. Let your rising flow from your resting. It can be one continuous flow. In the bathroom, letting go bodily wastes and washing can continue your sense of simplifying the day, clearing it of accretions.

Leave your TV and radio off, at least for the first few minutes. As you wash and dress, just participate in the flow of these simple activities, without judgment, without a busy internal dialogue that takes you "out" of the flow.

This simple presence in simple actions has a way of allowing more in-touchness and contentment with what is present already. We are less panicked and grasping for something "outside" to literally "occupy" us, such as a radio or TV program. Once we are calmed down inside and don't really need the TV/radio (or phono/tape), we can turn it on. Then it is an optional stimulant and not a compulsive one, and it is more likely to enhance or at least not dull or kill our underlying clarity.

Cross Currents, *op. cit.*, pp. 296ff.):
1. Insight and discernment: the ability to perceive intuitively the secrets of another's heart, to understand the hidden depths of which the other is unaware . . . to know immediately and specifically what it is the individual needs to hear.

Pay attention to your *body*. It is a tangible expression of your life. It is a vehicle for simple presence. Resentments, frustrations, fears, guilt, and pain from the past have a way of being stored up, "remembered," and reinforced by the body through various points of tension, stiffness, dullness, and sickness. These complicate our lives and block clear awareness.

What can we do to relax and alert our bodies?

Many of us jump too quickly for a cup of coffee or cigarette or other drug-like stimulant, just as we jump too quickly for the radio/TV. We need not feel so dependent on "taking something in," as though we did not have more natural resources of our own. Nicotine and even caffeine harm our systems. We all know or suspect this, but we will continue to rely on them anyway, if we know no better way to relaxation and alertness. Here are a few alternatives.

Breathing

Ways

Nothing we do is simpler, more basic, more readily at hand than our breathing. Focusing on particular ways of breathing can relax and energize us with amazing speed. An enormous variety of forms for controlling our breath have been developed over the centuries. Here are a few elementary ones that you can practice.

2. Ability to love others and to make others' sufferings his/her own, making constant intercession on their behalf more important than any words of counsel. The early Eastern Orthodox spiritual father Varsanuphius said, "I care for you more than you care for yourself" (*ibid.*, p. 312).

Deep Breathing

Take long, slow, gentle, deep breaths. Let your diaphragm (roughly your stomach area) blow up like a balloon as you inhale, rather than expanding your upper thoracic (chest) area. Put your hands on your stomach and you can feel this expansion happening. Shallow breathing from your upper chest can both indicate and reinforce anxiety, fear, and bodily tension.

Let your exhalation be longer than your inhalation. Slowing your outbreath can slow the speedy, greedy, grasping, anxious pace of the mind; it can raise up subtler, clearer, relaxing energy.

Practice this breathing before breakfast. You can do it even while still in bed. If you consciously begin breathing in this way soon after waking, you will find it easier to develop this as your natural way of breathing all through the day: while standing, lying, sitting, walking, working or playing. Whenever you are feeling particularly tense and blocked, check your breathing. Probably it has become shallow and rapid. Slow it down. Deepen it. You will find a new control over your panic, more space to be in and cope with the reality at hand, less panicky flight and uptightness.

Variations

If this form of breathing feels inadequate, there are countless variations. Here are three.

3. Power to transform the human environment, both the material and the non-material, including the ability to heal by his/her very presence, and to help others discern the universal presence of God. William Blake describes this power thus: "If the doors of perception were cleansed, everything will appear to

1. Hold your breath a few seconds before a slow exhalation. Repeat this process for several minutes, gradually increasing the amount of time you hold the breath, but without straining youself.

2. Block your right nostril with your right thumb, breathe in through left nostril; hold your breath several seconds, then release your right thumb and block your left nostril with your fingers, then breathe out through the right nostril; block the nasal passages near the opening rather than further up the nose. Repeat this process for several minutes, then shift to breathing in through the right nostril and out through the left (or alternate nostrils from the beginning).

3. From an upright sitting position, or else standing with hands on your legs (just above the knees), take several long, slow breaths. Gradually increase your rate of breathing, sucking in your breath and breathing out through relaxed, almost closed lips, expanding your diaphragm as just mentioned. This form of hyperventilation should not be practiced more than about half a minute unless you are under expert guidance. If you begin to feel faint, bend your head down toward your chest. The duration of the other forms of breathing mentioned above gradually can be expanded up to ten minutes if you like (no longer without guidance), but never force yourself to do more than is relaxing and energiz ing. You defeat right intent if you turn it into a competitive contest.

man as it is, infinite" (ibid., p. 305). Perhaps most of us do not need such a gifted guide at our stage of readiness. As Kallistos Ware puts it: "(People] close their eyes to the guides whom God is actually sending to them (because they expect a spiritual guide to be of a particular advanced type). Often their supposed

Whatever you do, avoid making a complicated, technical operation out of such breathing practices. At the very beginning these may have this edge. But it need not last, unless you get too involved and fascinated with them. Focus rather on their service to your simple openness. They are not important in themselves.[13]

Physical Posture

Spiritual Discipline

As Westerners we are used to being told that physical exercise is good for us. This means usually that it can help keep us physically healthy and develop strong muscles. Rarely is it presented to us as a spiritual discipline, as a way of allowing our bodies to be simple, open, clear channels of Spirit. St. Paul exhorted: "Glorify God in your bodies— God's Spirit dwells in you." One meaning of "glorify" is "reveal": *reveal* the Spirit in your body—reveal the subtle spiritual energy always present. Approached with this attitude, we are doing the same thing during physical exercise as the seeker of God's simplicity does any other time: in the wilderness (in this case of our bodies) preparing the way of the Lord.

Variations

The simple breathing exercises already described can

problems are not so very complicated, and in reality they know in their own heart what the answer is. But they do not like the answer, because it involves patient and sustained effort on their part" (*ibid.*, pp. 310-11).

[13]Breath or "vital energy" control has been given careful attention for thousands of years in India. You can learn more about "pranayama," as it is called there, through reading or working with an adept in this area. Some practical books on

help. So can a great number of physical postures. There are hundreds of variations to choose from. Most of them in our culture unfortunately emphasize violent movements of the muscles. For more subtly awakening postures arising from an appreciation of body-mind-spirit integrality and the evoking of balanced energy and simple presence, Eastern forms are more helpful. Many of them have the added advantage of being possible for us regardless of our age. One of the yoga teachers I know didn't begin until she was sixty, and she has worked with people in their eighties.

Far Eastern systems related to the martial arts more incidentally than directly, such as T'ai Chi Chuan and Aikido, are two valuable systems worth learning and practicing, if instruction is offered near you. Classes and books on Hatha Yoga, the ancient Indian system of physical awakening, are available much more readily.

If you decide to take instruction in one of these, be careful not to fall into the trap of seeing what you are learning as just a way of "feeling better," with a new set of imposed techniques. Some yoga teachers fail to focus on the underlying attitude of simple, transforming presence that the postures help to reveal. As long as *you* are aware of this underlying intent, though, you still can find it helpful to learn specific methods from such a teacher.

Simple physical postures can be learned from many available illustrated books.[14] If you learn on your own, be slow

---

yoga you may want to explore include: *Light on Yoga* by B.K. Iyengar, *Yoga in Ten Lessons* and *Yoga and God* by J.M. Dechanet, O.S.B., and *The Complete Illustrated Book of Yoga* by Swami Vishnudevandanda.

[14]Some good ones were mentioned in regard to breathing.

and gentle with yourself. Don't force your body. Striving to accomplish difficult postures is not the point. Simple presence is.

If at this point you just want to get started with a few very basic simple postures, here are some suggestions.

Sitting

Sitting isn't exactly a special posture, since we do so much of it anyway, but attentive sitting is relatively rare in our society and needs special mention.

Whenever you sit, let your back, neck, and head be in a natural, alert, straight line, yet not stiffly rigid. Relax your shoulders and stomach. This is the simple way your body really wants to be. Slouching is complicating: the body then is out of kilter and starts hurting. We restlessly, tiringly begin shifting around. We become distracted. Then we cannot be simply present for any length of time in anything we may be doing: whether praying, reading, eating, or relaxing. Chairs that support such posture sometimes are hard to find, but worth the search. When you do, sit forward on the chair, which helps your straightness.

Floor sitting is an alternative. If you're not used to this, here are two ways you can try:

1. Sit on your lower legs, kneeling, back up straight with a pillow between your legs to take the pressure of your upper body off them.

2. Sit cross-legged on the edge of a firm pillow or sleeping bag, with your right heel tucked up touching between your legs, and your left foot either on the floor touching your right lower leg, or brought up on top of your right leg, if you can manage it. In either case, your knees should be touching the floor to give you stability. If this is not possible, let one knee touch the ground. With practice, the other slowly will come down, too.

Let your hands rest palms up on your knees, with thumb and index finger joined in a circle. Or let your right hand rest in your left hand at the abdominal level. Or put your palms together resting against your chest.

These are classic positions for meditation and prayer. They are just as good for other purposes that involve long periods of sitting.

Bending Over

Stand straight but very relaxed, with feet about a foot apart. Especially relax your stomach and shoulders. Take a long, slow, deep breath. Maintain slow breathing throughout (don't hold your breath). Very slowly bend over from the waist, keeping your legs straight and your arms loose. When you are bent as far as is comfortable, stay there a few seconds with your head and arms loose. Then very slowly sense your body lifting itself, vertebra by vertebra, until you are upright again. Rest a few seconds, then repeat this move-

ment twice more. Throughout, let your mind be calm and present, with no sense of anything to achieve or think about. Let your mind slow down with the slow movement of your body. Let your attention stay in that movement: not ahead or behind it—just with it, wordlessly present.

Bending Back

Begin as above: standing straight but relaxed, taking a long breath. Then put up your bent arms, palms open (as a priest does during the Consecration of the Mass: the ancient Hebrew prayer position). Now slowly bend back from the waist as far as is comfortable, keeping your chin tucked down toward your chest. You may find your abdominal muscles begin to "shake." Let it happen. Begin to suck in air through your lips, taking strong, deep breaths. Continue for about half a minute. Then slowly bring yourself back to an upright position. This posture is particularly good for relieving pent-up anger and tension.

Eyes Following Fingers

Stand upright and relaxed. Stretch your arms straight out in front of you at eye level, side by side, palms down. Focus and keep your eyes on your fingertips. Slowly move your stretched-out arms to the left as far as you comfortably can twist your body (your feet don't move). Then, slowly, evenly swing your arms as far to the right as you can. Continue this

back and forth as long as you like, but at least four times. Keep your mind clear, wordlessly focused on your fingertips at all times. There is nothing to do but be fully present there, in that even flowing movement. Keep your breathing gentle; don't hold it.

Holding Your Knee

Stand and hold one knee with both hands clasped beneath it. Keep your eyes steadily on one spot a few feet in front of you. Pull your knee and body back so that your back and thigh are stretched. Hold this position as long as you like, but at least for half a minute. Then shift to the other leg and do the same thing. Don't hold your breath but keep it slow and gentle. Keep your attention wordlessly on the spot ahead of you. Sense a gentle confidence in the position. Watch how you lose that steadiness when your mind doubts, questions, wanders, complicates.

Relaxing On Back

Lie flat on your back with your legs straight out, feet about a foot apart, your arms at your side, palms up. Put your full attention like a laser beam of energy into your toes and feel them relax. Gradually work this relaxation up your body: your feet, ankles, legs, abdomen, stomach, chest, back, arms, wrists, hands, neck, mouth, eyes, forehead, crown of your head. Maintain long, slow, deep breathing. Spend extra time at places of particular tension until they are thoroughly relaxed. You can extend this form by slowly bringing your left arm up. Stretch it out behind you. Then stretch the whole left side of your body from toes to fingers for a few seconds. Relax, and slowly bring your arm back to your side. Then do the same with your right arm, stretching your right side. Then with both arms back, stretching your whole body. You can do this one before getting out of bed in the morning.

Rolling On Your Back

Sit on a soft rug with your knees pulled up and your arms enfolding them. Fall back, letting your folded knees and arms go up in the air, and rock forward to a sitting position again. Continue this at least six times. If you have difficulty rocking back to a sitting position, then hold your right ankle with your right hand and left with your left hand, instead of folding your arms around your knees.

Clear Presence

A very thorough discipline of postures would include enough to stretch and massage all parts of the body. A minimum daily discipline at least can relieve certain basic blocks that accumulate in the body and raise some of the subtle energy needed for simple, clear presence.

Movement

Slowly Flowing

Jerky, tense, rushed, grasping movements reflect and reinforce that kind of mind. The body and mind thus collude to block the simple flow of awareness. Pay attention to your movement. Earlier I mentioned rising slowly from your bed in a way that continues an even flow of consciousness. Continue this in the minutes of your "awakening" time and you will set a pattern for the day, just as you can with breathing practices.

Seeing

When you move slowly, keeping your mind present, not getting "ahead" of yourself, notice then how much more observant you become, how you see much that is going on in and around you that is missed when you become too speedy. Such attentive observation is likely to be simpler than usual, too: not complicated by compulsively grasping to get or avoid what you see. A body lunging forward trying to get somewhere stimulates a lunging mind trying to "get," too. A steady, alert body stimulates that different kind of even awareness.

Centering

Such flowing movement can be helped by sensing your

bodily center where it is: not in your head but in the middle of your body, a little below your navel; or you might prefer to sense the center in your heart. Allow your movement to be guided from these points whenever possible, rather than driven by your head. Then your body's balanced, graceful, simple wisdom can reveal itself.

Royal Bearing

Alan Watts once used a royal comparision for our moving around. A king and queen are the center of "where it's at," so they move with easy, royal bearing. They have no place to "get." They have already "arrived." Looking deeply at our lineage, we see that we are of the highest royal line: the royal image of God is in us—covered over, but indestructibly there. We need rush nowhere else to get it. We mainly need to attentively relax and dissolve the amnesia that obscures our true identity. Confident evenness in physical movement can provide a regular little jog to our tainted memory. When we know who we really are, life loses false striving and gains simple presence.[15]

[15]The great Sufi poet-mystic Jalal al-Din Rumi said: "The man of God is a king beneath a dervish's robe; the man of God is a treasure in a ruin" (quoted by Pir Vilayat Khan, Cross Currents, op. cit, p. 231). Such royal analogies for the divine image in us all are found in many spiritual traditions.

Chapter Five. Praying
What Is Prayer?

Into Love

Prayer is opening into Love; into that radiant and centerless Love surpassing our understanding and enfolding all of life. The truly holy person is wholly open in this Living Presence through every happening of the day. This is the root of that person's simplicity and consistency, and capacity to "see through" everything to this shared core that shines through all. The highest saint's life is one continuous prayer, one seamless participation in Holy Reality through all its forms.

Special Times

Special "prayer time" simply is an opportunity to give special attention to this opening. So much in our way of going through daily experience can cloud, warp, and close this natural openness. Without special time to cultivate it, we easily sink deeper into confusion and craziness. With careful, conscious attention, though, little by little it seeps into the happenings of the day. Instead of becoming more fragmented and defensive in these happenings, we see their underlying unity and their call for our open participation. We slowly become more capable of discriminating the incredibly dense and deceptive cloudiness in and around us from the always present sun hidden beneath.

Sky Burst

One of the most startling experiences for me is to be

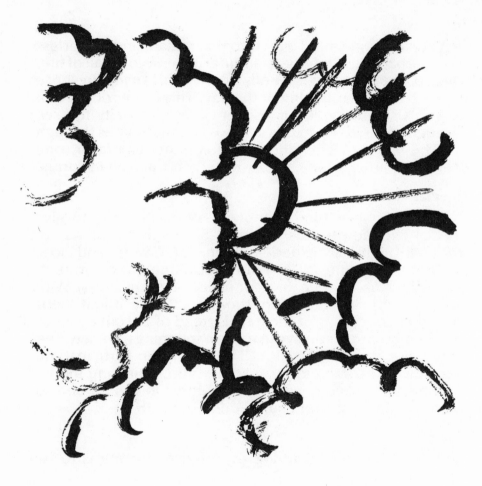

present in a thinning fog bank on the California coast and suddenly see the sun and spacious sky burst through. Everything that was dreary, cold, and dull suddenly takes on radiant sharpness and warmth. The open sky was there all along. But long days of heavy, dense fog have a way of dulling your memory, leaving you feeling that nothing else exists.

Prayer is a way of thinning the clouds that dull our vision. A way of cultivating trust in the ever-present Sun, no matter what our shallow eyes see at the moment. A way of helping us be in the fog but not of it, if you will—and thus capable of *insightful* compassion with others lost in the fog.

Inner Wisdom

When, where, and how we pray in this "special time" is unique for each of us. We need to listen to our own inner wisdom here. We are likely to find a dynamic quality to our praying: we slip into different times and different ways at different moments, as our lives and situations evolve.

Discipline and Spontaneity

We need an attentive weaving of discipline and spontaneity. Discipline—that is, committed times and ways of prayer, regardless of how we feel—eats away at the clouds that keep us from even wanting to pray. Spontaneity, on the other hand, saves prayer from that kind of compulsive routine that subtly turns it into a way of securing us *from* openness.

Here are a range of possibilities that you can weigh in relation to your own situation at this point in your life.

When To Pray

As a Way of Being

The goal always is what St. Paul exhorts: "Pray without ceasing" (1 Thess. 5:17). Pray as a way of being, be as a way of praying: steady holy openness. When we commit ourselves to prayer in this sense, then there is no "time out," no vacation ("vacating") from open attentiveness. We are not in a subtle bargaining relationship with God: "I will give you some time here, and then I will be free to give myself time there." That becomes a very complicated, split-up affair, a kind of on-going negotiation between an ego fiefdom and the overlord. Indeed, our ego-trips are not God. Yet God is in us. To focus on a relationship between our empire-building ego and God subtly can reinforce that ego. It becomes the "real I" constantly held up, a self-image with hard boundaries which must then be something to assert and protect. The ego becomes in fact the center, bounded by an unstable treaty with the overlord on the fringes concerning limits and powers of domain.

God Within and Without

We will find it much more true and helpful to focus on the union of God in us with God out of us: on the overlap between us; on the Spirit that is whole, though having relative "inside" and "outside" dimensions. Then the cloudiness of our confused ego-trips can be undercut. They no longer are the focus. They are mist that our prayer penetrates and lightens. We evoke and live out of a deeper self-image in God. Our egos, our whole personalities, become a dance and healing force rising from this underlying unity, rather than a counter-force leading us astray.

A Discipline of Hope

Given the ego-tripping toward which we are so prone—so strangely, sadly, powerfully driven—this deep reality is obscured. Only very intermittently, often against our ego-will, is it realized. Prayer without ceasing for us then is not a reality of steady openness, but rather a discipline of hope, a plow to cut through impacted ego earth, leaving room for the underground of simple unity to appear through the cracks.

Special Times

Special disciplines for "praying without ceasing" exist, such as the "Jesus Prayer," which I will introduce later. Even these disciplines, though, need special time at the beginning to help them "set" in us.

Such special times can be any hour of the day or night. Classic Jewish, Christian, and Moslem practices range from two to seven times daily. In orthodox Moslem countries all activity stops at three specified times of the day for prayer. Unless we live in a religious community, we will not find such societal support in the West today, which makes individual commitment and support of a few others that much more important.

Gatherings

I spoke earlier of the helpfulness of a "spiritual friend" for support and accountability. For prayer, a meeting with a small group of people regularly can be equally important. Such gatherings can range from formal liturgies in church on Sundays, to weekday house meetings. Meeting for a "one shot" retreat together can be energizing, but frustrating. Again and again individuals have come to me a few weeks after such an experience feeling too alone and unsupported to carry on a significant prayer/meditation discipline.

Meeting as a group once a week for two to three hours in my experience is ideal: more frequently becomes impractical, unless you're living together; less frequently just doesn't give you enough time really to get into it together.

Afternoons seem the worst time to meet for most people: that after-lunch heaviness/sluggishness gets in the way. Early mornings and evenings seem the best times.

Depending on your situation, you may want to consider a

regular meeting with work mates immediately before or after work, or during lunch hour. People in your family or other living situation may also be at a point where such regular gatherings are fruitful.

Personal Prayer

These meetings have a way of stimulating a daily prayer discipline between sessions. Some of us are more naturally night people or morning people. Our situations further influence what time is best to set aside. The advantage of early morning is the way it sets our attentiveness for the day. The advantage of evening is the way it reintegrates and settles us down for the night. It is ideal to set aside ten minutes to an hour both morning and night, giving more or less time as our situation allows.

Most important though is not the number of times or duration, but our deciding on *some* time and duration and sticking to it, at least for a trial period of a few weeks. This means that once we've decided to do it, we treat it like brushing our teeth: it is just something we "do," without agonizing over it each time. Brushing our teeth, once it's a habit, is very simple. So is prayer time. If we leave open a crack for "redeciding" every day, then it becomes complicated. We've undercut the very simplicity that prayer time can reveal.

When you feel resistance to prayer time, just lightly "see" the resistance, and get on with it. Don't judge your resistance. Don't even judge yourself if your resistance is so great that you give up your discipline one day. Judgment complicates our resistance and turns what is simple into a heavy struggle. Just gently notice what has happened, smile, and go back to your discipline the next day.

If after a trial period you find your resistance growing rather than receding, try different times and durations, or different content (which I will discuss later). If your discipline really gets to be too heavy a struggle, give it up for a while and watch what happens. In a few weeks you can reassess its value.

Becoming Natural

Always keep in mind that the underlying intent of your special prayer time is to enhance your simple awareness all the time. The goal is for prayer time to become less and less special and more and more our normal, natural way of being open: praying without ceasing.

Where To Pray

Special Places

Where shall I go from your Spirit?
  Or where shall I flee from your presence?
If I ascend to heaven, you are there!
  If I make my bed in Sheol, you are there!
If I take the wings of the morning

And dwell in the uttermost parts of the sea,
Even there your hand shall lead me,
And your right hand shall hold me.

(Ps. 139:7-10)

Particular places, like particular times, lose any ultimate significance when "prayer without ceasing" is realized—when God's Presence is seen without boundaries. There are no special spaces that can "contain" God. We can be free from such idolatry.

Yet such awareness is dim and erratic in us. Human beings everywhere instinctively seek out special holy places where they can realize holy presence more clearly. Think of where you go when you want to be in touch with reality more deeply: each of us will have a unique answer, unique places that are particularly numinous for us. There are certain characteristics most of us are likely to find in common, though. We seek a place that is quiet, secure, undisturbed, intimate, yet awesome enough to quiet the petty mumblings/grumblings of our minds.

Many of us head for mountain tops or waterfronts. There is a particular spaciousness in those places that encourages us to see farther than elsewhere. A perspective seeps in that awakens our sense of simple belonging in this flow of nature which bears and consumes our bodies. We become more porous to that usually dammed up spring of Living Water deep within us—that fresh stream washing clean the lens of

our perception and revealing an unspeakable Presence.

It is no accident that so many temples, shrines, churches, and monasteries are built on hilltops or waterfronts. On flat land, church spires instinctively rise to create their own mountaintops. Such constructed "containers" have a very controversial history as places for prayer. There are many biblical warnings against over-attachment to particular holy places and created objects. At the same time, particular holy places and symbols of Holy Presence are there and affirmed throughout. We find sacred space affirmed not just in the Bible, but in virtually all human cultures.

Attitude

The key for prayer space, as for prayer time, is our attitude. If we see God "here" and not "there," then we have God in a box. We lavish gifts on the box, we humble ourselves in the box, we are "good" in the box. Outside, though, it is different. We have a tacit bargain that I will "knuckle under" in the box where Big Daddy lives, but outside it is my box, my world.

Our attitude may be less crude, but amount in effect to the same thing. The result is a false splitting of reality, and of us along with it. "No man can serve two masters." An instability ensues as we wobble back and forth. One space fights for territory with the other. We invent endless self-deceptions to maintain the illusion of different spaces and powers.

Holy Spaciousness

If, on the other hand, we trust God's subtle presence everywhere, then we can allow special holy places to cultivate that simple trust. When I go to church, especially one that takes holy space seriously, everything draws me toward a clear awareness of Holy Presence: the quiet, the candles, the pictures, crosses, and statues, the altar, the pulpit, the tabernacle, the large open space with everyone together. My awareness of a special Presence here strikes my consciousness like a stone hitting water: my awareness radiates circles further and further out until "here" becomes everywhere. I see how inattentive I've been in other places. I realize the holy spaciousness that is there binding all spaces. This very particular church exposes universal sacred space. It heals the rifts of space created by my false consciousness. This special sacred space has a subtle way of freeing every space from fractured, confining, oppressive qualities.

Special Place

For special daily prayer time consider setting aside a special place in your house, apartment, or room (if you haven't done so already). This is an old custom in particular Christian as well as other deep traditions. Where it is and how it is furnished depends very much on our own situation. I have chosen a spot in our finished basement, the quietest place

in our house. I sit or kneel on a rug with cushions, facing a white wall partly covered with a wall hanging containing a "centering" design, a kind of mandalla.[16] On the floor near the wall is a candle,[17] a stylized crucifix, an ikon of Madonna and Child, and sometimes incense. I use this space for no other purpose than prayer/meditation, and related physical postures. Its familiarity from constant use has a way of settling me into prayer faster. There is less time taken in the old instinctive animal paranoia of "securing the space": checking out all the corners, making sure everything is all right, maintaining a taut edge of fearful watching. Being surrounded only with familiar objects designed to stimulate my deeper openness also saves my mind from too much curious wandering. Everything in view reinforces prayerful intent.

Children

Once in a while my young children come in unexpectedly during prayer time, looking for or wanting to ask me something. I find it important to accept these occasions simply as an extension of my prayer time and not treat them as "interruptions." Sometimes my two children (aged five and seven) sit down beside me in silence; sometimes we sing or pray or do exercises together for a minute. Soon with that abrupt spontaneity reserved for children they rise and go about other things, leaving me alone again.

I think it is valuable for children to sense such a place and

[16]Mandalla is the Sanskrit term for special forms of sacred design symbolizing reality, used in particular meditation disciplines. A cathedral rose window is a kind of mandalla.

[17]Be sensitive to the effect of a candle's color (or of other things around you). Different colors can affect our consciousness in different ways. In India there is a special science of color in relation to consciousness called chromatic yoga. I

period as a natural, almost casual part of their daily environment, even if they don't participate directly with you. Then prayer might more readily develop for them as a time of special openness and presence, within a single flowing Open Presence. Prayer is saved from its corruption as an imposed, artificial period dealing with some imagined separate world on the fringes of "real" life.

How To Pray

Stillness

"Be still and know that I am God" (Ps. 46.10)

When we become truly still, then prayer—opening into Love—happens. To be still is to be utterly simple:

The pure soul is like a lens from which all irrelevancies and excrescenses, all the beams and motes of egotism and prejudice, have been removed; so that it may reflect a clear image of the one Transcendent Fact within which all other facts are held.[18]

Much of what we normally call prayer ultimately is one kind of preparation for this spacious simplicity. Such preparation lights and steadies our interior lamps so that we don't miss the Master when He comes in the stillness of the soul's night. Preparation also helps us to absorb the shocks of

have heard it said that Christians had a greater understanding of color and its effects during the Middle Ages, expressed in the great stained glass of the period.

[18]Evelyn Underhill, *Practical Mysticism* (Dutton, 1973).

those moments of coming, so that their impact is clear and enduring.

Waiting

We cannot force or anticipate that "coming into our Own"—that homecoming—that awareness of the Kingdom. All we can do is attentively wait on the One we trust to appear. Not wait *for*—we wait for what we know. We wait in blind trust on the Surprising One beyond our shallow knowing. We wait attentively through every moment and activity of the day.

Here are two broad forms of prayer that can help prepare the way.

Prayer Of Solidarity

Suffering Present

Perhaps the most basic and steady prayer we need is one that involves us compassionately with the suffering present in and around us. Mahayana Buddhists have a tradition of regularly offering all the merits of their spiritual development toward the release from suffering of all sentient beings, and vow not to enter nirvana—heaven—until all have been released. Christians move in the same direction through constant identification with the cross—with the full involvement of the very Son of God in the world's suffering and for its release.

Interdependent

We are all in this unfulfilled life together, utterly interdependent. The mingling of our prayer energy for one another is the secret glue and salve and catalyst of authentic community. Without it, we become stuck on ourselves, with all the illusions and complications and added suffering flowing from that stuckness. The Master is not likely to be recognized when we are so clouded.

Praying Alone

Jesus Prayer

Over the past few years my most steady prayer of solidarity has been based on the "Jesus Prayer": "Lord Jesus Christ, Son of God, have mercy on me, a sinner."[19] This ancient, simple prayer is based on Paul's exhortation to pray constantly (1 Thess. 5:17) and on the Gospel cries of "Lord, have mercy." It was shaped by the early Desert Fathers and eventually became a classic form of prayer practiced widely to this day, especially among Eastern Orthodox Christians.

Historically the prayer has been flexible in its form except for the constant of the name Jesus ("Never say or do anything except in the name of the Lord Jesus"—Col. 3:17; "Everyone who calls upon the name of the Lord will be saved"—Rom. 10:13). In some historic uses it is done in rhythm with breathing, such as "Lord Jesus Christ" on the

[19]This is the fullest text; it often is shortened. For a very personal description of its learning and results, read *The Way of a Pilgrim*, written by an anonymous nineteenth-century Russian peasant. For descriptions by past masters, read *The Art of Prayer*, edited by Timothy Ware.

in-breath, and "have mercy on me" with the out-breath. I have found this coalescence with breathing very natural. The prayer at first should be done with full concentration for anywhere from five to twenty minutes at a time (no longer without guidance). Allow a short pause after each prayer. It is ideal to learn with an advanced practitioner, but such is hard to find.

Simply Being

Let yourself feel deep warmth, humility, and all other positive feelings that may come. Let all wandering thoughts and images gently melt into the prayer. Don't analyze the words, just let them happen in you, trusting their hidden truth.[20] After the words appear to have "set" in you, then they can be continued behind and between everything else you do during the day. After prolonged use the prayer can spontaneously "move from the lips, to the mind, to the heart," where it prays itself, so to speak. It can culminate in an utterly still, wordless, open, light-filled awareness, when the prayer, as Kallistos Ware says, "ceases to be something we say, and becomes something we *are*."

Openness

Even without these advanced gifts, I have found that regular use of the Jesus Prayer keeps my heart more open, centered, and warmly compassionate at times when I'm sure it otherwise would be more narrow and cold. The

---

[20]The Jesus Prayer is in the Orthodox tradition of the "hesychast," the person who has attained "hesychia," inward stillness or silence. As Kallistos Ware says, he/she is "the one who listens." Quoting another Orthodox writer he con-

prayer becomes a reminder of who I really am: an expression of grace, not fully realized, dependent on further grace for fulfillment; able to ask, that I might receive, as Jesus promised. The very asking implies a trust in life as ultimately merciful, full of grace, not dependent on my making things happen, but only on my attentive, open participation in what does happen.

Boundaryless

When I first began using this prayer I thought it was very selfish and distorting: compassion was supposed to be self-forgetful and other-directed. Here instead was a constant prayer that seemed to be focused on my isolated self. The very weighty tradition behind the prayer kept me with it, though. Soon I began to notice that its impact melted rather than strengthened the lines between me and others. I realized the truth behind a saying of the lama Chogyam Trungpa Rinpoché: "Compassion has no direction."[21] Compassion is an open warmth that is just there, a wave of divine energy at whose crest no boundaries, no "inside" and "outside," exist.

All in All

With me (and others I know who use it) the Jesus Prayer has a way of shifting focus through the day. As I see or read of someone suffering, the Prayer immediately begins, but

tinues, "When you pray, you yourself must be silent; let the prayer speak" ("The Power of the Name," *Cross Currents, op. cit.*, p. 124). *ibid.*, p. 346.

[21]Chogyam Trungpa, *Cutting Through Spiritual Materialism* (Shambala: Berkeley, 1976). He is the founder of the Naropa Institute and other Tibetan foundations in this country.

without reference to me. Instead, it becomes simply, "Lord Jesus, have mercy on him" (or her, or them), or simply, "Lord Jesus, have mercy." Where I once impulsively judged, ignored, or condemned the situations of others (and of myself, often enough!), now there is a deeper response where I sense my involvement with all that happens, and the suffering that lies beneath. I still get angry, hard-hearted, and hurt, but these moments are a little lighter now. Deep down I know the reality of suffering and grace is there, even when I can't feel and respond to these in the moment.

Illuminates Grace

So, rather than isolating me further, the Jesus Prayer has taken me deeper into the midst of the world, and yet without becoming lost in it. The Prayer, like a beam of light, penetrates to the grace there at the bottom of a situation and often saves me from becoming stuck at the shallower levels of awareness that incite paranoia, bitterness, depression and indolence. The beam of light is not so bright that I can understand easily a given situation and know clearly how to respond. Many times all I'm clear about is that the situation needs grace, and only God knows what form. I don't know specifically what to ask for or what to do; I can only ask for mercy, and do what I do, hoping the prayer will affect my openness to God's will.

Other Simple Prayers

The Jesus Prayer is not the only form of repeated simple prayer that can awaken our solidarity and attentiveness. Some people find it oppressive and difficult due to the warped meanings that were given to "mercy" and "Jesus" as they grew up.

In certain East Indian traditions there is a focus on "mantra," that is, repeated sacred sounds. The focus is more on the particular vibratory quality of the sound than (as with the Jesus Prayer) on its meaning. Different Sanskrit syllables are used for different situations, and for different personalities. "Aum" (or "Om") is the most well known and broadly used of these syllables, both the sound and meaning of which is seen as inclusive, an inclusive name of God, of Reality's Heart. Transcendental Meditation involves an elementary form of mantra, where particular Sanskrit syllables are assigned to a person according to certain broad personality characteristics; this mantra is said for twenty minutes each morning and evening.

Centering

The Cistercian monks at St. Joseph's Abbey in Spencer, Massachusetts, inspired by certain suggestions in the famous anonymous medieval contemplative work, *The Cloud of Unknowing*, have developed a related Christian form called "Centering Prayer."[22] It has three simple phrases:

[22]The name itself is inspired by Thomas Merton, who stressed that the only way to come into contact with the living God is to go to one's center and from there pass into God. A book describing Centering Prayer by a Cistercian brother, Basil Pennington, was published by Doubleday in 1977: *Daily We Touch Him*.

1. Close your eyes. Take a moment or so to become silent. Then offer a brief prayer for openness and trust, in your own words.

2. Let a simple, sacred word spontaneously emerge from deep within you that expresses your relation to God, your being in God. Slowly let this word repeat itself whenever the mind strays. If the word does not arise spontaneously, then introduce one very gently. Gently let it absorb everything else that clutters your mind: all your thoughts and images, all your memories, plans, worries, and hopes. There is nothing else to do during this time except say the word. Be very present in it.

3. After 20 minutes, slowly say the Lord's Prayer, or some other prayer to "ground" you. Pray in this way twice a day.[22] *

After learning this way of praying on a visit to the monastery, and continuing with it after, a startling thing soon happened. My "word" shifted a number of times. Each shift seemed to move to a deeper, clearer expression. Finally, while using the word "open", there was a spontaneous shift to "oh", simply the first syllable of the word. Suddenly I felt like I had struck the bottom. Yet the bottom was without boundaries, like going down the narrow confines of a well and reaching the open groundwater beneath its foundation. The sound burst all limitations of particular conscious meaning. There was vast space, awe, and deeply felt openness. No other word has every come to replace it.

When this happened I dimly sensed the origin of those

[22a]As Dom Thomas Keating says, this process "is the denial of what we most love and are attached to: our own thoughts and feelings. This is a kind of asceticism that . . . goes to the very roots of attachment to our superficial selves, our egocentric manipulative tendencies, and teaches us to let go. . . . This is detachment of the most intimate, liberating, and delightful kind."

open Sanskrit syllables for God, whose sound is more important than particular meanings. The Finest Reality slips through the crude nets of our finest meaning words, and we finally are left simply with some awesome sound. Perhaps this is why the name of God revealed to Moses, "Yahweh," was untranslatable, and why Orthodox Jews to this day go even beyond its sound to silence, forbidding that inner name to be pronounced or written.

Other Solidarity Prayers

Many other "prayers of solidarity" are possible. When I find myself grasping too hard, trying to make something happen, fearing it won't, I sometimes undercut this crowded pressing with a simple "Thy will be done," repeating it whenever the pressing closes in again. It is so difficult not to see yourself in the driver's seat, creating the world single-handedly. Our confused egos press us into that seat whenever possible. "Thy will be done" is one way to free ourselves. Free ourselves to be a little more organically involved with the flow of divine action. Free ourselves to be a little less mechanically involved in trying to construct the world in our own ego image.[23]

Snatches of prayers from the Bible, from prayer books, or from your own experience may have stuck with you and shaped your prayers of solidarity. These can be used as repeated words during the day, or they may be just exclamations of the moment.

---

[23]Though ego, our sense of self-importance, looks like an enemy here, it really is a confused friend. We need its strength in daily living. So be kind to it; but see it for what it is: an expedient construct, not an ultimate reality; a relative self-

Sense these prayers coming up from some infinite depth. Even formal prayers such as the "Our Father" can take on fresh awareness if we sense "kingdom" and "will" and "heaven" unfolding out of life, rather than dropping down from some separate "above."

Sometimes we find ourselves spontaneously "talking with the Lord." St. Teresa of Avila called this "mental prayer": "Friendly intercourse, and frequent solitary converse, with Him who we know loves us."[24] If we are going to chatter inside, it is better to do so mindfully as mental prayer, rather than mindlessly "talking to ourselves." As mental prayer, the chatter more likely will lead to simple listening and holy perspective; as self-to-self chatter, it is more likely to lead simply to more chatter: narcissistic, anxious, and narrow.

Praying Together: Formal Liturgies

Graceful Support

Perhaps nothing reinforces our solidarity more than mutual willingness to gather together for prayer. A sensitive layman once told me that gathering for worship on Sunday mornings was the only time his family gathered regularly with other people for more than entertainment. Indeed, corporate worship is a precious opportunity for supporting one another's deeper aspirations and identity. It is a time when the simple thread of grace can be revealed through all that is.

image, not our ultimate image in God, wherein lies our real worth and enduring identity.

[24]*The Life of St. Teresa of Jesus* (Image paperbacks, 1960).

The Ways

Unfortunately this opportunity easily is lost in the way corporate worship often happens. Worship leaders and congregants alike bring all kinds of clutter into that hour, clutter that obscures the subtle Presence and leaves us distracted, scattered, judgmental, dull, striving to please, wanting to be pleased, gossipy, and all the other surface vibrations that complicate the time. It is no accident that probably the purest worship I have experienced was in a humble contemplative community. You could sense the inner simplicity of the monks carried into the liturgy from their daily lives, a simplicity that let them just be there innocently present in the liturgy (though this innocence even for them, I think, still is erratic). Their simplicity overflowed into the form of the service itself: unaccompanied plainsong, plain white habits, simply designed space. An unadorned corporate presence and commitment seeped through the words and actions, allowing an even, rhythmic flow. That liturgy evoked a magnetic spaciousness that gently drew monk and guest alike into a solidarity beyond our many differences and tensions. We were present to one another at a level of shared belonging beneath our fluttering egos.

This simple presence is possible for us through many diverse liturgical forms and communities. We can influence its realization both in the form of service itself, and in our own way of being present, regardless of the form.

Liturgical Form

Suggestions

Here are a few selected suggestions regarding form. Since laity and religious are so much more involved in planning worship services these days, I address these suggestions to them as well as clergy. Even if these are not possible in church, they can be done in services held in our homes and other places.

Silence

Allow a rhythm between silence and sound. People have little opportunity for corporate silence in our society. Stilling surface sound allows us to "listen" in a fresh way. There is nothing we "have" to hear or do when we become silent together. That allows us to relax attentively into just "being" together.

Since few people are accustomed to valuing this silence, a certain fidgeting and silent chatter with ourselves often fills what seems at first like an empty and threatening void that we must somehow fill. To avoid such "killing" of the living silence, the congregation can be taught some specific ways of being silent. Some of these ways are mentioned in the next section on "Prayer of Quiet."

Silence during the service can come at the beginning, after each Scripture lesson, after the sermon, between

prayers, with Communion, and at the end. The words and actions in between are likely to be heard and absorbed much more readily when such space is provided. Sometimes it can be helpful to "cover" the silence with carefully chosen music designed to evoke particular feelings and images, as many churches do. But there should be total silence at least sometime during the service, with no musical props. The Society of Friends (Quakers) long has demonstrated the value of such corporate silence: it is the very heart of their liturgy. As with them, we might well leave space at some point for persons to share spontaneously certain concerns and prayers that rise from their silence.

Raimundo Panikkar offers this insight into silence: "Only a word coming out of silence is a real word and says something. . . . And the Silence was made Word—and began to Speak. . . . The relationship between silence and word is a non-dualistic one, and neither monism nor dualism will do justice to their penetration. . . . There is not the one without the other, and it is the one which makes possible the other. They are neither enemies nor incompatible. Of course, there are escapist silences and repressed silences, as well as empty words and nonsensical chattering; it is only such non-authentic words or silences that are at variance. Any authentic silence is pregnant with words which will be born at the right time. Any authentic word is full of silence which gives to the word its life. May our words be always words of silence and our silence always the virgin womb that does not speak, just because it has nothing to say" (*Cross Currents, op. cit*).

Song

The Hassidic rabbi Shlomo Carlebach once reminded me that people must be separate to talk, but they can sing together. Singing is one of the most corporate acts we make.

Listen to Carlebach: "When someone is crying, and he tells you why he is crying, you may say he is right, or maybe you'll say he is wrong. But when someone just cries without words, you're so filled with compassion! Therefore, in our tradition we just sing. No words—because maybe then we'll get back to the oneness of the world; because words separate us, but the melody is so good" (*Cross Currents, op. cit.*, p. 348).

We can be much more simply imaginative than we often are. We don't always have to make people fumble through hymn books, lock their heads in them, and try to get through hymns with melodic ranges often too difficult for the average singer and with verses that go so fast and cover so much ground that we don't know what hit us.

Simple presence beneath and through the words sometimes can be evoked more clearly when people simply sing the refrain of a song, or even just an antiphon (a one line verse) over and over, with one or more singers singing the rest. There also is value in the old practice of "lining," where a leader sings a line, and everyone else sings it after him/her such as a psalm or spiritual. This slows it down and gives us space to absorb the underlying mood. In the black church tradition there is room here for individual variants in lining that allow unique personal expression woven into the corporate context.

Plainsong (Gregorian) chanting and its modern variants perhaps are our closest equivalent in the West to Eastern mantra. Though there is significant meaning in the words, the real impact for me is in their sound and flow. No kind of music so smooths and clears the ruffled waters of my mind. One of the great advantages of much plainsong is its simplicity and small vocal range. I am a terrible singer. But I can chant. Everyone can chant. It also has the advantage of requiring no instrumental accompaniment. Finally, its relative lack of bouncy rhythm requires a kind of special attentiveness to corporate pace and mood. This attentiveness is hard, and its requirement sometimes puts people off. But its reward can be a more awake and shared mind.

Plainsong somehow expresses that kind of prayer that is beyond what we know, the kind St. Paul calls the Spirit's sighs too deep for words (Rom. 8:26). It moves us beneath the abstract rationalism or overly self-conscious sentimentality of many hymns into a non-rational (not irrational) and non-sentimental (but deeply felt) presence.

Space

Pay attention to the corporate space. Is it cluttered with distracting and unconnected odds and ends? Is there a simple focus? Does that focus draw one deeper into reality, or is it a literal store-bought metal cross or sentimental picture that somehow blocks, distorts or dulls people's awareness?

Must the space be stuffed with pews or even chairs? Wouldn't a great, rugged open space with cushions allow people to be together much more simply and intimately, with some chairs around the edges for those who really need them (as in many Russian Orthodox churches)? Pews and chairs were rare phenomena in churches until the last few centuries. To me they have a way of cluttering, complicating, and freezing the space. At least you might try a compromise, as I know at least one church has done successfully: take out some of the front pews, put down a rug there, and give people a choice. That opens the space at least a little more.

Sermon (Homily)

It is not necessary always to fill the sermon time with words. After the Scripture lessons, you can give the people silent time to work and pray on their own. The lessons, after all, are their own sermon. Doing this once in a while can wake people up from the temptations of becoming merely consumers. Our society already provides too many opportunities for falling into the status of shadowy, well-entertained, passive consumers.

Guiding personal reflection on Scripture is another way. There is a form of this attributed in outline to St. Teresa of Avila that I have used many times both at sermon time and in personal prayer (as well as during guided retreats). It requires a pictorial kind of biblical passage to be fully valuable.

Usually I begin with a very brief summary of the lessons and their connections. Then I ask all present to sit up straight, take several slow, deep breaths, relax, and close their eyes. I continue over about a twelve to fifteen minute period with the seven steps of the meditation, leaving space between each.

1. Put yourself into the Scriptural scene with all your senses . . .

2. Let the scene fade, except for you and Jesus . . .

3. Over the next few minutes, be with Jesus alone. Let everything happen as spontaneously as possible . . .

4. Now let that experience fade. Feel a deep sense of appreciation, of thanksgiving, without words . . .

5. Sense your partnership, your full indestructible belonging, with the rest of life . . .

6. Now sense that your time in that interior dialogue (step 3) will have some kind of impact on your life . . .

7. Finally let all thoughts and images fade. For the next several minutes let your mind be as clear and calm as possi-

ble. Just be simply present . . .

If the situation permits (usually in an informal setting), I give people an opportunity to share their experience (voluntarily) with the person next to them for five or ten minutes. Usually a rich array of experiences are revealed. People often get in touch with deeper layers of awareness than they thought possible, especially in so short a time. I find it important to emphasize the final stage of the meditation since many people tend to treat is as an anti-climax. If I understand St. Teresa, it is this last stage that is most important—that moves toward the Prayer of Quiet for which all else is preparation; to this prayer I will devote careful attention later.

Announcements and Continuity

If in the midst of a gripping play someone suddenly darted onto the stage and yelled, "Now turn to page nine of the script—John will marry Julie, and they will move to New York," we all would lose our involvement in the flow of the drama. Liturgy is common prayer, a congregation, not an audience, calling for even more personal involvement than a play. Breaking the flow of involvement with directions, observer-like descriptions of "what we are doing now," and information about the coming parish supper clutters our awareness and prevents us from going beyond a surface consciousness.

Information can be given in the bulletin, and orally after the service if it really is urgent. Service directions can be in the bulletin or on bulletin boards.

The more continuity there is from week to week, the more the forms can sink into our consciousness and the less external directions are needed. The words and actions become ours, rather than alien forms imposed from the outside. With long use they can wear so thin that their surface disappears. Then they become transparent windows through which their inner truth appears. For this to happen, of course, the words and forms need to be inspired and tested, such as the ancient Kyrie, Eleison (Lord, have mercy), and the Sanctus (Holy, holy, holy . . .), and the words of institution ("In the night before he died he took bread . . . "), and great collects, and other moments of the Spirit's work.

I realize this runs counter to current experimentation and constant shifts in liturgical form. There indeed is value and need for such. Changes can correct old errors. They can shock us into fresh awareness. I have been heavily involved in "liturgical renewal" for fifteen years. But constant change, I've learned, is very complicating, very self-conscious, and thereby an inhibitor of simple presence.

A recent informal survey in a group of Episcopal parishes concerning the years of experimentation with new liturgical forms had a very interesting result: a great many people were not so concerned with *which* form was chosen, but that *some* form be chosen and relatively stabilized. The authentic side of this reaction, I think, is precisely the instinct to center down together in common prayer, and not be scattered and fumbling on the surface through ever strange forms.

Personal Response In Liturgy

More Suggestions

We cannot always control the forms of liturgy. We can, though, be attentive to the way we are present in any form. Here are a few suggestions:

Settling Down

Arrive a little early so you have time to settle down. When you're seated (or kneeling), take a few long, slow breaths. Sense the points of tension in your body and relax them. Watch your mind: see its scatteredness and anxieties. Don't identify with them: smile to yourself; gently let them go.

As your eyes fall on other people, notice how your mind is attracted or repelled, how you latch on to someone in fascination, or judge someone in displeasure. Before falling too deeply into these traps, pray for those people. It may be as simple as "Lord, have mercy." Such a prayer can free us for a deeper quality of solidarity and equanimity with the people around us, a result very different from the kind of relationship given out by our impulsive ego desires and repulsions.

Simple Presence

As you become settled down in these ways, you will notice a capacity to be more simply present *in* the words and actions of the service. You will become less of an outside observer watching and acting in an external show. When such simple presence happens, stabilize it, let it continue. There is no need to "step outside" again and "see" what's going on. The need is to be in the flow of what's going on. Surrender your protective outside observer and let yourself go into it fully, until there is no "it" left—only the communing.

Participating

Gestures, our physical involvements in the service, are the points of our fullest participation. Especially let yourself be present in these. When you bow or kneel or cross yourself, when you walk into the church or up to the altar, when you light a candle or incense, when you offer Peace to another, when you put money in the plate, when you receive bread and wine, don't pull away inside. Don't separate and see yourself doing something. Just do it! Be fully present "in the middle" of the gesture, with nothing left over. Let the gesture express and reinforce your simple, open participation in the Body.

To do more is to complicate gesture. We do more many times, of course, We are conditioned to do more than the simple. But notice the "more" when it happens. Don't judge it; just see it, gently let the "more" go, and simply be present again. If you do this even for an instant, life for that instant will be together, as it really is, reconciled.

If you are in your liturgical gestures in this way, you might find it easier to be simply present in your gestures elsewhere, too: in your handshake, your touch of a child, your wave goodbye.

Focusing

When your mind scatters, you can find some spot for your eyes that will help you be recollected again. The most helpful focus for me at such times is a candle flame, which is present in most liturgies. Its bright, steady, living quality has the capacity to dissolve the darting fragments in my mind and bring me to clear one-pointedness. If you do this, don't think about the candle flame. Just let your mind wordlessly merge with it—so fully that there is no sense of any space left between: you are in the flame and the flame in you. This will happen spontaneously when your mind is fully present, with no split-off observer left in you watching and no thoughts interpreting. Such presence is likely to last only an instant, but that instant will leave a long, spacious echo in your mind.

Informal Prayer Together

Rhythms

Earlier I mentioned the value of informal prayer/ meditation groups. In most of the groups where I have participated over the last few years there has been a rhythm of ingredients over a two to three hour period that has served both the solidarity and simplicity of the group. This rhythm includes:

1. Silence on entering the prayer/meditation room.

2. Sitting in a circle (optionally on the floor or in chairs), with a candle in the middle to help gather our wandering attention.

3. A brief opening ritual of some kind to gather us into prayer. Usually we chant a long "shalom" with a slow bow, our hands together, bowing in respect and trust for the Spirit among us.

4. About ten minutes of breathing or physical postures to open and relax our bodies.

5. A guided prayer form of some kind, ranging from scriptural passages and intercessory prayer through the methods mentioned in the next section on quiet prayer.

6. A period of silence, usually about half an hour, focused on the form of guided prayer, always aimed ultimately at interior silence, openess, and compassion.

7. A short period of silence for journal keeping.[25]

[25]Groups are referred to the journal-keeping methods of Ira Progoff (a psychologist heavily influenced by Carl Jung), summarized in his book *At a Journal Workshop* (Dialogue House, 1975). His approach represents the most thorough

8. Optional shared reflection on our experience during the silence, or during the week since we last met. Sometimes particular intuitive questions are posed at this time, too, such as "What is the Kingdom of God in our midst?" We do not fall into elaborate discussions over such questions, but in silence allow one or two words to arise, and share these without comment until all have shared.

9. Ending as we began, with a chanted shalom and bow.

Friend Pairs

Often the groups have divided down from their normal size of about eighteen into "spiritual friend" pairs. Sometimes we reflect in these pairs before reflecting as a total group. Some friends meet occasionally outside the group for reflection, support, and prayer.

Settings

Informal prayer together in some simple form is possible in many settings: with friends, families, or work mates, in homes, hotels, locker rooms, prisons, hospitals, at the scene of an accident or natural calamity, at political events. One of my most powerful experiences of such prayer happened in the middle of a civil rights demonstration in the early 1960's. A small group from my church joined hundreds of other people in an amusement park the denied entry to non-whites. Gathering together in late afternoon, we

---

form I know of not only for recording thoughts, feelings, events, memories, and dreams, but for helping these to be carried forward into greater clarity and integration from a subconscious level.

opened the prayer books we had brought and read Evening Prayer together as naturally as possible. Never had the prayers, psalms, and lessons lived so fully for us. Certain words that normally pass by without a nod now exploded with meaning and strength. A TV camera passing by picked up part of the service, which shared its offering with thousands of others, enfolding the demonstration into the perspective of the Kingdom.

The civil rights and peace movements were filled with the poignancy of such praying moments. The black Baptist tradition in particular taught me much about the naturalness of prayer and action woven together into one expression of open concern.

Prayer of Quiet

Grounding

Prayers of solidarity ground us in the matrix of life: its giving and receiving, its interweaving, its sharedness, its integral givenness. They broaden our identity so that we come to realize we do not exist in isolation, but as a unique, fleeting, grace-filled meeting ground of intricately woven energies.

Imageless Prayer

This grounding is culminated in what can be called

"prayer of quiet," or imageless, wordless meditation. Here we come to realize the grace-filled solidarity of life in deeper and deeper layers of consciousness. Our whole being slowly and sporadically becomes flooded with an awareness of the Kingdom in our midst. Quiet prayer is the culminating prayer of the great contemplatives of the Church[26]—and of other deep traditions. Its full development is the greatest and rarest of gifts.

Simplification

The key to quiet prayer is simplification—fuller simplification perhaps than our usually cluttered minds even can imagine. A fully simple mind is calm and clear. It is present in reality as it is, before that reality is screened by our thoughts, feelings, and images. It is the mind of the Cloud of Unknowing, the mind that cannot be "peaked at" by our usual faculties because it appears only when these are quiet, surrendered. Such a simple mind is a prayerful mind when its intent is opening into ineffable Love, when its trust is in the Heart of this Love. Quiet prayer is an opening of our whole being that relinquishes every faculty we would cling to.

St. John of the Cross, one of the masters of quiet prayer, describes it in this way:

> *God's wisdom to which the intellect must be united has neither mode nor manner, neither does it have limits,*

---

[26]I am using quiet prayer in a more inclusive way than sometimes is found in its classical descriptions. Here it covers all the qualities of awareness from interior stillness through union: adoration, recollection, quiet, spiritual betrothal, spiri-

neither does it pertain to distinct and particular knowledge, because it is totally pure and simple. That the two extremes, the soul and the divine wisdom, may be united, they will have to come to accord by means of a certain likeness. As a result the soul must also be pure and simple, unlimited and unattached to any particular knowledge and unmodified by the boundaries of form, species, and image. [27]

Such words push us to the limits of our awareness—and beyond. Words always have been a little ridiculous and clumsy in trying to describe what can be grasped only in first-hand experience. Perhaps then we need not worry about understanding the conceptual descriptions of the masters, but get on with cultivating our own first-hand appreciation.

Spiritual Guides

It is very valuable to have a spiritual guide with such prayer. Spiritual directors in Christian tradition came into full-blown existence with the early Desert Fathers and Mothers. Spending so much time alone in silence, they experienced many strange and difficult things in their Christ-inspired journey toward simplification. Spiritual fathers and mothers arose to help less experienced persons steer a sane and holy course through these happenings.

tual marriage (to use St. Teresa's stages). But in these few pages I will make no attempt to describe these subtleties of awareness. For their description, cf. such a work as Evelyn Underhill's *Mysticism* (Meridian, 1955).

[27]*Ascent of Mount Carmel*. In *The Collected Works* of St. John of the Cross (Institute of Carmelite Studies, 1973, pp. 151-52).

Unfortunately profound guides for the interior journey into quiet prayer have not been cultivated very carefully in recent times, and we are not likely to find one (as I have lamented earlier). We can find a spiritual friend, though, whose basic sanity and concern we trust. On a regular basis we can meet with that person and share some of our experiences, as I have recommended earlier. The very sharing may give us enough perspective and support to avoid the worst temptations, pass through our fears, and continue the journey.

Some Methods

Here are a few methods that can help us get started. You can experiment with different ones for a while, but eventually it is important to select one and maintain it as your central practice for some months or even years. Each method is an elevator that in time, with grace, can take us into quiet prayer. No method is important in itself. As is said in an old Eastern saying, after the raft takes us to the other shore, we no longer need it. And the raft is carried by the Spirit.

Constant Prayer Forms

Already I have mentioned the Jesus Prayer, Centering Prayer, and other "constant prayer" forms. These can move us into quiet prayer in time.

External Visualization

Let me use this practice to speak in greater detail about the process of quiet prayer. I mentioned earlier the value of focusing on a candle flame during liturgy. There are many other external forms you can choose. Any form in fact potentially can give your mind a focus and clear it of unstable wandering and heaviness. But some forms are better than others. The best forms also will have a certain simplicity, naturalness, and balance. The Greek cross is a good example, where the cross-beams form a balanced crossing, rather than the unbalanced one of Western Christian tradition. A replica of a Greek or Russian ikon, or of a particular rose window, are other examples.

In Eastern mandallas there are great varieties of carefully balanced geometrical and symbolic forms representing the basic nature of reality. If one of these draws your mind toward stillness, you can select it for focus. Or you might select a piece of bread, a bowl of water, a leaf, a flower. You might choose a mirror and watch your own image, focusing on or between your eyes. Each form is a facet of the same diamond, a window into our minds, and ultimately into the clear awareness of quiet prayer.

Sit about two feet from the image, at eye level (closer or further if comfortable focus requires it). If possible let it be the only object in view. Relax your attention into the object. Let everything that comes into your mind be absorbed by it.

For now, that image is all of reality.

Don't resist the thoughts and images that come. But don't stop them—let them pass on by and melt into the image, and brighten it. There is nothing you need do except be present—fully present in the image. The clearer, more "empty" your mind becomes of other things, the more your sense of distance from the image will collapse. If this participation continues for a long period, you may find that the image suddenly turns into other images: people and scenes familiar from the past, or perhaps unknown ones. The images eventually may burn up into bright light, or disappear all together if your mind becomes really still. Perhaps you will hear new sounds and voices, or speak in tongues. You may feel great terror, or great bliss, or great calm.

All this skirts the edge or falls into quiet prayer. The more your mind becomes still, confident, spacious, simply present, the more you become aware of your existence as grace: all is given, all is sustained in the Holy One. Even devilish images and feelings that appear become but the near side of a coin when we heed them not, maintaining a steady mind through them. Their other side emerges, dissolving them like bubbles in water, revealing the Loving One. The great masters describe an awareness even beyond this: where there is neither bliss nor terror, just clear presence—Utter Simplicity.

Such full awareness I think can develop only with the greatest commitment of energy and confidence in God beyond all our images of God, and beyond all our desires. We probably will not be gifted with this full awareness; most of us in this lifetime are not able to bear the price of "nothing left holding anything anywhere," but this is all right. We don't have to have (or let go of) it all now. Our waiting on God must be a most patient waiting, so patient that each moment is treated as sufficient for now, without need to jump ahead, grasping for more than is given.

If you maintain a steady discipline of such meditation, you are likely at least to ease the heavy load of clutter in you. You also are likely to emerge from such meditation with a warm compassion that frees you to be with people and situations with a more intimate quality of caring, understanding, and lightness. Fears are reduced, and we are thus less prone to avoid facing into hard situations. Desires are lightened, and we are thus more content and free in the present moment.

Of course, these benefits have a way of being very sporadic. That stubborn clinging to our deluded "old Adam" is very powerful and takes over again and again. Purgation involves inescapable agony and frustration. Patience with ourselves (as well as with others) again proves the prime virtue.

Internal Visualization

The same process mentioned with external visualization can be taken within. For example, after focusing on a Greek cross for about twenty minutes, close your eyes and picture it in the middle of your head, at the height of your eyes. Don't try to "force" it to be present. Just believe that it is there, whether you see it clearly or not. Again let every thought and feeling melt into that visualization. Hold it very still. Let it be very bright. With a still mind, it may become three-dimensional and extremely clear. When it is fuzzy and wobbly, probably the state of your mind is being reflected. The image is something like a biofeedback process that puts you in touch with your current mind state and gives you opportunity to calm its cluttered busy-ness, for the sake of the Empty One.

Continue this for twenty to forty minutes (or much longer, with guidance).

In certain Eastern traditions, particularly Tibetan, this form of meditation is carried to very elaborate and sophisticated extremes. The goal though always is a simple awareness beyond the visualization—that is only the vehicle.

Even "vehicle" may be misleading, since the method really doesn't take you anywhere else than where you already are. Perhaps "atmosphere" is a more precise word. A method provides an atmosphere through which always present simple awareness can appear.

Sound

When a sound occurs we usually allow it to distract and narrow our attention. This need not be. Sound can be a "way in" to quiet prayer.

Sit very still with your eyes closed and listen. When a sound comes, just let it be sound. Don't label it: "That is a chair squeaking"; "That is a horn blowing." That limits the sound to less than it is. Every sound is a vibration that in a sense is infinitely inclusive. Left free of labels, that vibration has a way of opening and clearing our minds.

This result is enhanced further if we free the sound from judgment as well as interpretation. Don't respond with "That is a good (or bad) sound." Sound is just sound before our judgments come and separate us from it. There are a number of ways we can respond to sound. One way is to merge with it: let the sound fill you and everything around like a wave of fresh water passing through. This is applicable to everything from a bird's song to the screech of brakes to Beethoven's Ninth Symphony.

Another way is to stay in the silence surrounding the sound, behind the sound, in the middle of the sound. The instant sound happens; allow your mind lightly to stay in the silence that always is there with the sound.

We can make sounds as well as listen. Such Sanskrit syllables as "om," "ah" and "hum" have powerful vibratory qualities that we can draw out and repeat over long periods of time. Or we can use resonant words like "shalom" and "alleluia." When you do this, let yourself be fully present in the flow of the sound, with no "observer" left over, and with no anticipation or looking back. The sound for the moment is all there is, an expression of reality that is sufficient. Let it

fill every part of your body and mind and environment, with no remainder.

Such chanting is best done with the reinforcement of a group doing it together. But this is not necessary.

When you stop chanting (or singing), stay in the silence following for at least twenty minutes, with your mind as still and clear as possible. Notice any attempts of your mind to grasp for something more: a passing sound or thought or image. Gently let those restless graspings go. Your mind needs nothing now but quiet. Trust that the Spirit lives in that clear, spacious place present before your mind reaches out. There is nothing of value to get by grasping now. So be still. Not frozen or rigid, but still like the surface of a becalmed sea.

Scripture

Most of us are conditioned to read Scripture very analytically: this means such and such; it is related to that historical situation; it applies to this in my life; etc. Certain passages, though, lend themselves as well to an intuitive approach that can feed quiet prayer.

This is especially true of certain verses from the Psalms and from declaratory statements of Jesus, but suitable verses can be found throughout Scripture. The verse beginning this section is one:

"Be still and know that I am God." Others would include:

"In quietness and trust shall be your strength" (Is. 30:15). "I am who I am" (Ex. 3:14). "Whoever loses his life for my sake will find it (Mt. 16:25). "Having nothing, but possessing all things" (2 Cor. 6:10).

Take such a verse, sit down, close your eyes, and repeat it slowly, a minimum of twelve times. You can do this in rhythm with your breathing if you like, as with the Jesus Prayer. Silently moving your lips may give it emphasis. Don't step outside of the verse in order to "do" something to it: to understand, judge, etc. Just stay present in the flow of the words. After you stop, sense the verse remaining there subliminally, just below the surface of your consciousness.

You can remain present in meditation with a clear mind now if you want to take the time. Or you can move directly into your daily activities, sensing that verse remaining there, in a kind of clear, true space always present. It can surface spontaneously now and then during the day. This surfacing can come in the middle of any situation. Sometimes it comes in a way that you suddenly "realize" the truth expressed by the words: this realization flashes through you like a bolt of lightning. In that instant you have no more concept of the verse, but a living, intuitive awareness.

Trailing verses out into interpretive meanings can be extremely valuable, but such a way alone also can starve our intuitive way of knowing: one concept leads to another, and there is no end to the labyrinths that our minds can build.

Intuitive awareness moves in the opposite direction: instead of moving out into conceptual associations, our mind moves back into a simple awareness that allows the verse to be realized in a pre-conceptual way.

Perhaps the ideal is to combine the two: begin with the conceptual: the historical context, the meaning of the words, their possible application to our lives. Then "simplify" the verse; just let it be there in you.[28]

Such an intuitive ending is not unlike the use of koans, mind-boggling riddles, in Zen Buddhist tradition. The koans are meant to lead the mind into a quality of awareness, of unscreened participation in reality, that is blocked when the conceptual mind is spinning its webs.

Image Surrendering

As our minds seek for the spacious awareness of quiet prayer, there are subtle blocks along the way that need special attention. Chief among these perhaps are those clinging self-images that are reborn every instant. These come so fast, in fact, that normally we are not aware of any space between them, just as the individual frames of a film move so fast that we are not aware of the space between. But the space is there, wherein we are fully naked, without a shred of self-concept or boundary.

The greatest trust is needed to allow this final surrendering of what we usually believe must be kept if we are to live.

---

[28]This process is akin to the classic scriptural meditation form called "lectio divina," which includes four steps, pictorially described by a medieval Carthusian monk: 1. "like putting solid food into one's mouth" (lectio—sedulous reading); 2. "breaks and masticates it" (meditatio—intellectual meditation); 3.

When this happens, there is no hard ego left, for the self-images that support ego have been relinquished. We come as close as possible to being in reality as it is—rather than outside in our images of it. Here is the dark night of the soul, and the radiant light of awakening. Quiet prayer, simple presence, is fully realized.

This is no "abnormal" state of being. It is there naturally all the time, but there so quickly that we miss it; we are asleep even to its possibility. Our striving for a separate empire, a hard separate ego, our distrust and fear of anything else—these deep urges drive us to stay asleep. Only very gently and attentively and patiently can we lighten this resistance and be free for the grace of such naked presence. Even if we never actually realize this presence—even for an instant—just trusting that it's there can be enough to lighten our self-image attachments.

This can be such a frightening, difficult and subtle process that a guide, or at least a close spiritual friend, is essential in its advanced stages.

There are many unpredictable ways by which grace leads us into such awareness. There are some methods (simple in concept, not practice) that I can suggest, based on my experience with Tarthang Tulku Rinpoché, that might help you move on the path toward seeing and relinquishing hard, clinging self-images.

"acquires a taste" (oratio—prayerful appeal); 4. "is the taste itself which gives joy and nourishes (contemplatio—contemplation). (Taken from the Letter from Guigo II, the Carthusian, to Brother Gervase on the contemplative life, called Ladder of Monks ("Scala Claustralium").

Staying Between Thoughts

When you are in silence, stay "between" your thoughts as much as possible. That is not "dead space." It is very alive. As you see a thought or image begin to arise, immediately and gently move "behind" it and stay there. If you don't catch it soon enough and it becomes full-blown, then don't identify with it. Treat it like a cloud passing by. Note it, and let it go.

Self-Questioning

There are a series of questions you can ask yourself during silence:

1. "Where do thoughts come from?" Don't try to analyze this. Just watch carefully for half an hour or so, as your thoughts arise, and "see" where they come from, without any interpreting concepts. This process both saves you from identifying with thoughts, and helps you to stay in that spacious awareness there between thoughts.

2. "Where does the observer come from?" Usually we keep an observer handy, some split in consciousness that allows us to stand outside what is happening and observe, judge, protect, comment, manipulate. Watch the observer with intent, wordless concentration. If it dissolves, stay there in that unobserved fresh quality of "single-mindedness" as long as possible. If another observer

appears, then watch it in the same way until it melts.

3. "Where does self-image come from?" This perhaps is the most subtle question possible. Watch your "sense of self" lurking just beneath your surface consciousness. See how you cling to it for a sense of identity. See how it shapes the way you see and act. It is a relative sense of self that often is valuable in daily life, conditioned by myriad influences in our personal and genetic past. But it is not *ultimately* "you"—it is not the infinitely more spacious image of God present in you (though this image is not *ultimately* separate from that relative you, either!).

Very lightly, gently let that self-image dissolve. Trust that it will rise again when you need it. Now—in your meditation—you can let it go. Stay there in that spacious mind. Even-mindedly, confidently stay present through any sense of threat or strangeness. Remember that lyric: "Like a tree standing by the water, I shall not be moved." There is nothing ultimately to fear, except believing in the fear more than in God through the fear—on its far side. If fear comes, ask yourself:" *Who* is afraid?" This might help you loosen your identity with the fear.

Again I strongly recommend a close spiritual friend or guide to check base with regularly if you undertake these ways of clearing the subtler idols of your mind for any prolonged period of time. They are "hard work"—calling for extremely careful attentiveness. Without someone to be accountable with, we are not likely to maintain the concerted energy needed. Don't force yourself to go further than you feel ready. Your fears as well as your indolence will pull you out again and again. That is inevitable. Don't complicate the pull-out by judging it. Just see and accept evenmindedly whatever happens. Each time, though, whenever possible, gently let yourself "stay in" just a bit longer.

You will find that such an approach in time both cultivates simple presence, and loosens your attachments to particular self-images and observers. We will find ourselves able to move through relationships and events of the day a little more calmly and freely, a little less bound to protect and assert a particular image, a little more free to respond with open appropriateness in a given situation. But sporadically! Don't try for perfection: just for deep acceptance of what is given.

Putting It All Together

Daily Discipline

Prayers of solidarity and quiet fit hand and glove in a daily discipline. Like any hand-and-glove fit, though, it comes out a little differently with each of us. In my own "special prayer time" daily I usually begin with some breathing and physical posture exercises. Then I use some prayer of solidarity: this may be the Lord's Prayer, or intercessions for particular people, or simply a wordless sense of identification with the suffering and grace alive in the world. Then I will move into some method of quiet prayer for most of the time. At the end I usually sense briefly the people and situations with which I will be involved in the coming hours, open my arms, and allow as much wordless, warm, energetic openness as possible to rise up toward that time.

A Very Light Task

All of us must discover our own best use of prayer time, and be open for the Spirit's way of welling up at all hours of the day and night. This is not a "heavy" task. It is a very light one: barely touching the attractions and fears of the day, dancing through them with a disarming inner smile, and restoring this interior smile quickly when we fall into heaviness anyway.

There is nothing really to lose in the day; that is a happy law of physics: nothing is lost. There is nothing then ultimately to protect. There is nothing really to gain during the day, either. That is a law of God: the Kingdom is in our midst (though hidden and needing fulfillment), when we have eyes to see. Since there is nothing ultimately to gain or lose, except the heavy chains of our desires to gain and our fears of losing, then there is nothing left for the day except open compassion. When we realize (not just conceptualize) this, even for an instant, for that instant we are free, and God is glorified.

Chapter Six: Relating

Five Responses On Seeing a Flower

- Ah!
- Oh, beautiful—I want it, but I will let it be!
- Oh, beautiful—I want it, I will take it!
- Oh, beautiful—I can sell it!
- So?

Dorothee Solle[29]

Oneness

Relating is like breathing. In one sense, the air we take in is the same air we breathe out: one reality, the same on the inside and the outside. But in another sense, the air comes out differently: the chemistry has shifted from oxygen to carbon dioxide. So our breath comes not just as same air to same air, but as one distinct entity meeting another.

In one sense we are in all without ultimate boundaries. There is no real in and out. Everything is in. There is no stable, hard relating, just a common, fluid being. That is the first response to the flower above: simply, "Ah!"

Distinction

And yet there is distinction, a sense of in and out. An impact and a reaction. An interaction. All but the first and last response express these.

Insignificance

The last response is the dull one: nothing of significance

[29]*Christianity and Crisis*, June 7, 1976 (Vol. 36, #10).

really is there. So the flower is ignored—not really seen.

The Day

Moving through the day, we respond to whatever is there in one of these ways. Or perhaps in the opposite way concerning the middle three:

"Oh, terrible—I don't want it, but I will let it be!
Oh, terrible—I don't want it, and I won't take it!
Oh, terrible—I don't want it, I can't sell it!"

So we relate during the day through our attractions and repulsions, or a spacious "Ah!" or not at all.

Simplicity

Let's look at each of these ways of relating briefly, and find their simple side. I will use only a few examples as we go along, but keep in mind the enormous breadth of relationships there affecting us (and we them) all the time, whether or not we are conscious of them:

—the great network of interacting cells in our bodies;

—the infinite relationships with nature: animal, vegetable, and mineral;

—relationships not only with the people we are with during the day, but the subconscious, on-going relation with those who have gone before us (whether a close relative, a known statesman or religious leader, or an unknown saint);

—the subtle energies/beings that we cannot capture in words, but to which we give such names as Chi, Prana, Holy Spirit, Love, Christ, and Demons.

AH!

Presence

In that first flash of meeting there is always an "Ah!"—a quality of simple presence. It comes and goes so fast that we usually miss it altogether. That flash of presence is likely to reveal itself when we are not primed to get or fear something. Thus we are more likely to allow it breathing room when we are on vacation than in the middle of work. In that "looser" time we are slowed down a bit. We let life be a little longer before doing something to it. Sitting peacefully on the porch in the evening we find ourselves just present "in" the sunset, or in the play of children, or in our friend's hummed tune.

Agápe

This "Ah!" moment is the seedbed for that kind of loving that we have no English word for and so have to borrow from the Greeks: agápe. Agápe is being with and for another, but without attachment: without wanting and fearing. Agápe is the roomiest kind of loving, because it lives in that spacious place where all is accepted, and all is sufficient. At the same time it is the most intimate kind of loving, for where there is nothing to hide there is no distance left between us. In deep prayer agápe is present, as it is at the pinnacle of all relationships. Agápe is the fullest expression of the Holy One in daily human life. When such love lives in us, for that moment we are Home.

Caring Presence

I vividly remember experiencing that love toward the end of a three-day silent retreat many years ago. I had been struggling desperately the first two days: restlessness, anxiety, internal chatter relentlessly plagued me. On the third day, while walking in the woods alone, I was flooded with a sense of caring presence that dissolved every internal struggle. So complete was this that the struggle itself seemed as if it had been a mirage, a shadowy phantom battle on the surface of a sea that suddenly became radiantly transparent, transmuting the battle into glowing light. I was left utterly peaceful, satisfied, joyful, fearless, and in gentle love with every living thing around. For the rest of the day, before the old battle slowly reappeared, there was an intimate lightness, a taste of Home.

I saw a different form of this love in the experience of a close friend once. While still a young child, his parents were divorced. He experienced very little caring and rapport with

either of them. As a college student he developed a special relationship with a professor who also was a Presbyterian minister with four children of his own. My friend called on the professor and his wife at all hours of the day and night, unconsciously testing their concern. He had never known a deeply caring relationship marked by the kind of unconditional acceptance he found with this family now. Eventually he changed his middle name to theirs, and informally was adopted by them.

One Thanksgiving he invited me to spend the holidays with him and his new family. I tasted what he already had fully digested: an almost casual acceptance and joy together with an openness about weaknesses that such acceptance allowed. It was not a "perfect" family. But it was rooted in a tacit confidence in the way Reality is. Those people simply and directly expressed the Gospel: God is for us, so relax and let love happen through the struggle.

Acceptance

In Japan I remember hearing a young man tell me why he had joined the Church: he said it was the only place he had experienced acceptance for who and what he was unconditionally. Everywhere else he was accepted only on his merits and social conformity (would that the Church always left that impression!). Again, agápe appears. The "Ah!" is full blown: the first fresh participation with another, before judgments appear. The on-going participation there between and behind judgments.

Givenness and Coherence

Judgments, of course, do appear. Our egos go to work in all their helpful and crazy ways. But if we remember the always present "Ah!" and its full-blown fruit of agápe, then our judgments and consequent actions will keep an edge of freedom and perspective. There will be room for remembering the simple givenness and mutual co-inherence of relationship.

Oh, Beautiful (Terrible)—I Want (Don't Want) It—But I Will Let It Be!

Minding

Now we take the first step beyond the innocent presence of "Ah!" Our minds go to work on the relationship with judgment and decision. "That woman (man) is beautiful. I want to possess her (him)." Our mind grasps and pants like a hungry mouth drooling with desire, or like a dry mouth locked tight when we judge: "That man is crazy, I want to avoid him."

Free Choice

Here is our first opportunity for decision. What will we do

with this sense of desire or repulsion? Tarthang Tulku Rinpoché once compared this moment to holding a bowl filled with liquid feeling. We have the choice of pouring it into us (for repression or expression), or else spilling it the opposite direction onto the ground. But the choice must be made in a split second. Our freedom lasts just that long. Unless we "catch it" fast, we will miss the choice and just fall into a compulsive action one direction or the other.

Letting Be

When we decide to "let it be," then we have poured the impulse to possess or avoid onto the ground. We have allowed the person to be. We are free to be with them or not, but without the burning desire to possess or slink away. Their beauty and craziness are just there. We still see and feel these (they are not repressed or hidden). But they are realities that are but lightly touched.

Light Touch

A friend once told me he carries around a dog-eared scrap of paper in his wallet with this verse concerning the "light touch," by William Blake:

He who binds to himself the joy
Doth the winged life destroy.
He who kisses a joy as it flies
Lives in eternity's sunrise.

Blake could have written the same thing concerning our compulsion to run from sorrow: from the painful and ugly and crazy, or at least what we have judged as such.

When we are most at peace in ourselves, when our confidence, acceptance, and commitment to simplicity as a way are at their height, then we are free for such a light touch. That is when agápe, non-attached (not de-tached—out of touch) loving, is carried from the "Ah!" right through our judgments to the other side. Our judgments then help our appreciation of a person (her beauty, his seeming craziness), but leave a clear, calm, open, warm space in which we can stand with that person, without dominating personal need to get or shun.

This is a rare state of grace! When we see its living quality in another person, it evokes deep trust and inspiration in us. When we allow it for ourselves, we see our freedom at its most mature. We come closest to revealing the image of God in us.

Oh, Beautiful (Terrible)—I Will Take (Shun) It!"

Possession

The frightening story of Narcissus is always with us: falling in love with his image in the water, he fell in to embrace it, and drowned. He tried to possess what he already had, and lost everything.

The more we lack that quality of inner confidence and acceptance, the more we seek to possess these from the outside. We drive to fill ourselves with relationships and honors and things. We see our need stamped on the face of each of these; we horde and pile them up day by day. Depending on them for identity and meaning, we drown ourselves in their image.

Trying to possess a relationship is like trying to hold water in our hand. We cannot do it. There is a fleeting, slippery quality that refuses to be held. We can vow fidelity in a relationship, but we can possess the "other" in it only for an instant. The plucked flower quickly fades.

When we believe we must possess to live, then we live in perpetual fear. We fear losing what for the moment we seem to possess. We fear that what we don't want—the terrible, the ugly, the crazy—will possess us. We are empty vessels trying to hold the pure water and terrified of being filled by the impure. The impure we turn into enemies ruthlessly guarded against. The pure we coax and seduce and charm and wangle to get.

Sharing Fullness

When, on the other hand, we trust that the fullness of truth always is present there both in and around us, merely waiting to be uncovered, then relationship becomes very different. There is nothing of ultimate significance that we must get which we do not already have. And there is nothing that must at all costs be shunned in fear of its possessing and destroying us, because the image of God in us is indestructible and full. We are not empty beings needing to be filled by relationship. We are full beings free to share and evoke from its hiddeness this fullness already present everywhere.

Sense of Loss

It is so easy to forget this already full presence. I can be aware of it one moment, and suddenly lose it the next, as though a dark cloud suddenly appeared and covered the sun, leaving me cold and empty. Then I am driven to find warmth, and to dread not finding it, dread being left alone. Such feelings drive me compulsively to take and shun. Feeling like Adam driven so far from the Garden of Eden that the memory of who he is fades completely, I let crazed strivings and fears sink me into ever murkier waters.

Skylight

So what can we do when this happens? Most important I think is to allow a tiny skylight to remain somewhere subliminally in us, the tiniest hole that we do not cover over, even though we cannot go through it at the moment. That hole is our abiding fragment of authentic awareness, a divine trace that allows us faintly to know the craziness we are in and not fully become lost in it. That skylight is our escape hatch back into Sanity. Perhaps it is maintained with faint words like the

Jesus Prayer, or just wordlessly sensed.

When particular emotions arising out of our drivenness to get or avoid grab us, there are other little things we can do to lighten them.

Go Backward with the Emotion

Let's say that something just happened to block our getting or avoiding something and a wave of anger has begun to rise. If we "catch" it fast enough, we can "pour it on the ground" and let the situation be. But if we don't, and the anger is there full blown, then just "watch" it a minute. You need not try to analyze it: "I am angry at so and so because of so and so." As Suzuki Roshi so succinctly puts it[30], such attempts at interpretation are complicating "extras" that can trail the anger out in all directions.

Instead of moving out with mental associations, move backward: reduce the anger to its simple state. Let it be no more than it is: a wave of energy passing through you. If you let it be just this simple, then that narrow, churning negative energy is transformed into open, positive energy. This quality of energy makes you very alert and aware. It expands that tiny hole of deeper, spacious awareness. Then you find yourself responding far more powerfully, helpfully, and openly in a relationship.

Go Behind It

Another little way of dealing with a cloudy emotion is to

---

[30]Suzuki Roshi, *Zen Mind, Beginner's Mind* (Weatherhill, 1970).

go "behind" it the moment it has arisen. Close your eyes and picture yourself in front of you as you look now: all tightened up in that emotion. Then move quickly, with great concerted energy, *behind* that image of yourself, where it is very spacious. Stay there. Unless you are very attached to the negative emotion, it will dissolve, or at least lighten. That same energy is freed to become more positive and clear, able to serve the relationship.

Ask Who Is Feeling This Way

Ask yourself: *Who* is angry? This will help you lighten your identity with it. Then there is a little space between you and it, and you need not be consumed by the emotion.

Give It Away

If the desire to take or avoid is very strong, we can "give it away." Pick the flower, but give it to someone else. Cling to or avoid someone, but offer up the relationship in prayer, or in talk with a confidant. That can loosen its hold on you.

Fall Simply and Watch

When all else fails, then fall into the trap and don't worry about it! That may sound crazy, but when we struggle in quicksand, we only sink deeper. So possess or flee. Don't complicate it by poor-mouthing yourself or rationalizing your actions. Just do it. But watch! See what is happening. Watch from that tiny hole of awareness barely visible in the center. For now, the watching is enough. Accept what is happening. It just is. If your acceptance is deep enough, it will have a strange way of lightening our actions—making their continuance a little more optional.

All relationships reflect the interdependent, magnetic quality of life. All relationships seek and respond to the call of Love. But as Ernesto Cardenal reflects, our seeking and responding, our quality of loving, is not yet sufficiently free and pure. "Our attachments are like drinking salt water," goes an old Buddhist saying. We think it will cure our thirst, and instead it drives us mad with thirst.[31] "But he who drinks of the water that I shall give him will never be thirsty again" (Jn.4:11-15).

God is our only homesickness. God calls to us from the innermost depth of all creatures, and He is the chant that echoes in all creatures.[32]

Authentic relating then is relating in God. We can enjoy all relationships and fear none in God. We will enjoy none and fear all if we mistake the creatures for God, if we fail to see that subtle Presence already there in and around us. This Presence need not, cannot, be possessed. It already simply is, here and now, equally present everywhere, free for all, waiting to be celebrated. When we realize this, then perhaps we realize with St. Paul what it means to "have nothing, yet possess all things" (2 Cor. 6:10).

[31]Lama Mipham in Golden Zephyr (Dharma, 1975), p. 27.

[32]Ernesto Cardenal, To Live Is To Love (Doubleday, 1974), pp. 27-28.

Oh, Beautiful (Terrible)—I Can (Can't) Sell It!

Sometimes we reduce relating to using. "What profit can I receive from this relationship?" "To what use can I put it?" Such an instrumental view receives powerful support in our highly competitive, profit-oriented society. Everything has an exchange value. Everything (and maybe everyone) has its price. Looking over the people with whom we spend our time during the week can be very unsettling. If people have money or power that we or our organization needs, do we give them a great deal of special time? If they have none, do we cut them down to a passing nod? Do we see the beauty and living quality of a piece of land or garden, or are they just dead nature, inert matter, worth so many dollars, manipulative into this efficient shape or that profitable form? Is this book a "way of getting ahead" (for you and me), or is it in some way an end in itself, a way of living life now, sufficient for now?

Everything of course does have utilitarian value. We can be thankful for this possibility. "The laborer is worthy of his hire."

Economics is a reality we must pay attention to, for the sake of our own and others' material well being. Every relationship cannot be of great "I-Thou" quality. But neither must it be exclusively utilitarian. Harvey Cox long ago in *The Secular City* helped us see that we can have a simple human "I-you" relationship with the plumber, the cashier, the waitress, by paying a little attention to their humanity and situa-

tion in the moment. Nothing big: just a little sensitivity to their having an intrinsic worth far beyond their job capacity. This doesn't mean we don't have a right to resist exploitation, when others don't see *us* any more deeply than our profit value to them. But even then we can have an underlying awareness of how much they as well as we are missing when life is reduced to so little.

Softening

We seem to be on the edge of a little softening in the society now concerning material and status profit. It is still important—still too important—but the emptiness is just a little more apparent, and fewer people seem willing to reduce the value of life primarily to such profitability.

When we find ourselves spending too much time on "salability" in relationships, it's good to take some time out just to be present with people and flowers and life. Even in prayer we might weight ourselves more toward just being there, "wasting time with God,"[33] allowing ourselves to appreciate life as it is, finding the "Ah!" again.

So?

Inattention

So many times I walk dumbly down the street, my mind occupied with trivia, missing everything important. My wife turns to me and says: "Did you see that?" "Did you notice so

---

[33]A favorite phrase of Father Mark Dyer, Missioner of the Episcopal Diocese of Massachusetts, responsible for priestly spiritual formation.

and so's anxiety when she spoke?" "Why don't you listen?"

We miss so very much every day, every moment—so much that is right there in front of our noses: of beauty, of need, of truth. Earlier I spoke of the value of slower movement in helping us see more of what's there. Along with this we can pay attention to how we crowd our minds with planning and remembering, the future and the past, which keep us from seeing what's present right now.

Narrowing

Sometimes when we're with people (especially "important" people) we "freeze up," we narrow our perception down to what pleases and gets us through the time together. When we notice this happening, we might relax a little, allow a more spacious consciousness, allow a little more room for surprise and less for shriveling self-conscious control. When this doesn't seem possible, don't judge yourself. Simply chalk it up to your human frailty. Let it serve your solidarity with others' frailty. Then you might be a little more accepting of their craziness, too. Our human solidarity is just as much in our failings as in the image of God that shines through on their other side.

Ebb and Flow

While standing in the Pacific Ocean surf recently I was struck how well its ebb and flow mirrored our ways of relating. The sand could not exist without that surf, nor would the surf be the same without the sand. They interact constantly, feeding and stroking each other with shells and seaweed, feeding others in turn through these gifts. Their relationship spans the gamut of violent possession and calm caressing and indifferent separation, of beauty and profit and loss.

A Scottish-American friend once told me a saying about mythical Scottish stinginess: "Scots always cast their bread on the incoming tide." We all try to do this. But the bread we cast never comes back the same. There is grace in simply accepting the mysteries and unpredictabilities of relating, and in remembering its simple givenness, like our breathing in and out, that leaves us in the end just there present in the "Ah!" of it all.

Chapter Seven: Serving

"Oh, Terrible—I Can Help!"
"What Do You Do In a Country
Where Enough Is Always More?"

Helping

Dorothee Solle didn't include, "I can help" in her ways of responding to relationship, but it is clearly a special sixth response.

Serving is a natural way for nature and man. It happens all the time, whether we are conscious of it or not. Don Juan, the Indian shaman in the Mexican desert whose teachings fill the books of Carlos Castaneda, once told Castaneda to construct a trap and catch a rabbit for dinner. He did so, and was just about to kill the rabbit when their eyes suddenly met, only inches apart. There was a quality there that stopped him. He froze. Don Juan with great authority shouted,

"Kill it! Its time is up . . . The rabbit's death is a gift for you in exactly the same way your own death will be a gift for something or someone else.[34]"

A Vision

A close friend of mine once had a vision of Jesus during a scriptural meditation. Jesus was sitting on a rock perfectly still in prayer. My friend in the scene sat on a rock nearby trying to become still in order to meditate. But he was extremely restless. He just couldn't settle down. Finally he gave up and began to walk away. Just as he turned to leave, though, he suddenly noticed that Jesus had become very

[34]*Journey to Ixtlan* (Simon and Schuster, 1972), pp. 114-15.

restless and agonized. My friend sat down again and now found he could sit perfectly still.

Such is the complementarity of life: of suffering for another so s/he[35] can be free of suffering, of giving so another can receive, of receiving as another gives.

The complementarity goes on endlessly:

—being male to serve a female, and female to serve a male; being both male and female inside ourselves, allowing one to serve and balance the other;

—having divine potential to serve the finite flesh ("You shall be as gods"—the Holy Spirit dwells in you"), and human finitude to serve the Holy One;

—having muscle and brain and feeling to care for others: man, animal, plant, and stone, and having these others with qualities that care for us.

Alone we are nothing. Together all forms one interpenetrating reality.

There is a sad twist: when we ignore this truth of complementarity, and treat ourselves as a central empire to be served, and turn man and nature over to this exclusive self-service, then a cry of agony resounds in heaven. Freedom is misspent. Great suffering ensues. A web of distorted acts builds networks of vanity, violence, and delusion, and such iniquity is visited upon the children "to the third and fourth generation." Such sin, our shared karma built up through many lifetimes, spreads like a cloud of poison gas,

[35]The word "s/he" is a contraction of she and he, one little relief in the vast sea of male imagery for the generic human in which the English language forces us to swim. I will use s/he as a pronoun for God as well as persons. God is beyond person, yet, as Paul Tillich once said, God is *at least* personal, since that is the highest, most intimate state we can imagine. God's Personhood is inclusive of male and female. Listen to the great fourteenth-century English mystic, Julian of

engulfing all so none can see. We become the blind leading the blind.

Action

This is the catch in our service. Given this deceptive cloud, this strength of ego's haunting phantoms, how can we *really* help? How can we avoid simply adding scales to the blindness already there? Our very desire to help may be polluted by a childish desire to please (and thus be well thought of), or to assert power over another. How dare we say, "I can help!"

That question is raised again and again in the Bible. A sense of calling to service is accompanied repeatedly by a sense of personal unworthiness. But the divine press from within to do it anyway wins out. A deeper confidence takes over: a sense of "I will guide you—fear not—my Spirit will speak through you—I will show you the way." This reassurance, combined with exhortations to love one another as we are loved, prompts us to action.

Preparation

In Eastern traditions this press tends to be qualified more than in the West by a deeper sense of need for special preparation to serve: meditation and many forms of renunciation designed to reduce ego confusions and willfulness. Out of such preparation grows more insightful compassion.

Norwich: "Jesus Christ . . . is our Very Mother: we have our Being of Him—where the Ground of Motherhood beginneth. . . . As verily as God is our Father, so verily God is our Mother; and that shewed He in all . . . the Might and the Goodness of the Fatherhood . . . the Wisdom of the Motherhood" (from Julian's *Revelations of Divine Love*, quoted by F. C. Happold in *Mysticism*, Baltimore, 1963), p. 325.

But even in the East charity is seen as an essential way of life from start to finish—as a primary means of "ego reduction" in itself. So in the end East and West unite to press us into service, into fulfilling the yin-yang, giving and receiving complementarity of life.

How

But how do we serve? Especially how do we *simply* serve? We are pressed from every side with opportunities and challenges: in our work, our family life, with friends, with materially and emotionally destitute people, with animals and plants, with social, political, and economic structures crying for justice. Then there are those cries from within: our own bodies and minds crying for nourishment.

Attitude

As with our prayer and spiritual development as a whole, it is our basic attitude that is most important, the same attitude needed for everything else: patient attentiveness. Just as we do not wait for God but on God, so we do not wait for but on others. Even those who are closest to us remain surprising mysteries. If we think we know others and their needs perfectly well, our form of service is likely to be oppressive: we will act out of our assumptions and give them what we think they need, which more than likely is a projection or our own needs.[36] Our greatest service to

[36]Thomas Merton in his own way elaborates on this danger, and integrally ties together awareness and action, when he says: "He who attempts to act and do things for others or for the world without deepening his own self-understanding, freedom, integrity, and capacity to love, will not have anything

others will be to give them "space": to provide an environment which will help free their spirits to unfold and their bodies to heal.

Environment for Helping

A psychiatrist friend[37] once told me that a doctor never heals, s/he only provides an environment for healing. With a cut, for example, the doctor cleans the wound, puts the cut edges side by side in their natural place, and puts on a bandage to give it rest. That is what we can do for people: provide an environment that clarifies, cleanses, and lightens whatever messy situation is there, brings together what is torn asunder, and gives secure room for rest. This environment doesn't "make" healing happen. It *allows* it to happen.

Simple Serving

That same psychiatrist also told me of his experience with a wise, old faith healer one time. She told the doctor that he had special healing powers. But she wouldn't send her dog to him, because he thought *he* could do the healing.

We cannot heal. We really cannot even help. All we can do is be patiently attentive: watching, being open, for the way grace might come through us in a situation. That grace comes through in ways we are not even aware of much of the time. It is not really dependent on our conscious, clear awareness and action. Patient attentiveness is more subtle

to give others. He will communicate to them nothing but the contagion of his own obsessions, his aggressivity, his ego-centered ambitions, his delusions about ends and means" (*Contemplation in a World of Action*, Doubleday, 1971).

[37]Dr. Gerald May, a co-worker in the METC Shalem Institute for Spiritual Formation.

than that. It is allowing something to flow, to come through, to happen, even when we have no clear sense of its helpfulness: only the vaguest intuition. Perhaps all we really can do in a situation is be open, almost innocently open, encumbered by as few assumptions as possible. Such simple presence frees us to be in the unique situation, with the person at that moment, in an intimate but not crowding way. What we do then we simply do: with a kind of spontaneity that involves minimal calculation, and minimum memory (i.e., memory of "I" did something and "he/she" should be grateful). Our act becomes like a flash of lightning in the situation: it arises in an instant and dies almost before it is seen.

Vowing

In a complex society where everything is infinitely rationalized, churned over, thought through, and its consequences weighed, such simple serving is not easy. Nor is it easy when inside of us we are building and protecting little empires of time, goods, pleasures, and knowledge. This difficulty is one source of that historic instinct toward "poverty, chastity, and obedience" found pervasively in Eastern and Western spiritual traditions. Such vows, when seen to include both internal attitudes and external "holdings," can simplify our lives and leave us more simply present in a situation, with nothing to get or protect from it. Cassian, the great early inspirer of Christian religious community, spoke of "detachment from possessions, sin, and, finally, from all that is not God."[38] Louis Bouyer, the contemporary interpreter of Christian spiritual history, declares that such "counsels of perfection" are meant for all, not just for monks and nuns, though almost inevitably more erratically and selectively for those without communal support.[39]

Sitting Loose

If we are not called to such radical community at the moment, and we are making our way through all the accumulations of American life, perhaps our simple presence with others will be served best by *sitting loose* to what we have. Our goods, knowledge, plans for getting this and that: well, there they are. We enjoy them. We want them. But we don't really need them. They are expediencies that are part of the dance of this life. They are not its essential heart. They can bring delight and point us to the Giver, but in themselves they do not bring fulfillment. They are good, but not worth fearful over-protecting, not worth the blocking of our simple presence and sharing with others, or with the Other, who is our Heart.

Ignatius Loyola

Ignatius Loyola, founder of the Jesuit Order (Society of Jesus), once said that if his order (which he had struggled so long and hard to establish) suddenly was dissolved, it would take him about fifteen minutes to re-establish his

[38]Louis Bouyer: *Introduction to Spirituality*, p. 191.

[39]*Ibid*.Non-attachment is very tricky here. We need to recognize that we can become subtly attached to "poverty, chastity, and obedience," too, and find ourselves as bound as ever.

peace of mind. That is an example of sitting loose! We do what we do. We put great energy into our sense of vocation and delight and goods and service. But we do not cling tightly. We don't drag all that around with us like an ever-expanding, heavy costume that must be shown off, preserved, and identified with at all costs. The costume is expendable. We are more free than that. When we believe this, we can enter situations with our brothers and sisters (and our own hearts) a little more nakedly present.

Gandhi

Such looseness serves our patient attentiveness in the larger societal scene as well. We become a little less engrossed in our own holding and getting, a little more aware of the injustice, shoddiness, and oppression there in those social-political-economic structures in which you and I and our neighbor swim every day. And we become a little more free to take action. How we respond will depend on our own resources, situation, and vision. Just as God and our neighbor maintain a core of mystery and surprise, so does social process. Thus patient attentiveness again is the key. Gandhi was fond of repeating, "One step is enough for me."

Gandhi, that great bridge between East and West, who cut through so much of the truth and falsehood in each, still offers vision for simple societal service. "Civilization," he once said, "in the real sense of the term consists, not in the multiplication, but in the deliberate and voluntary reduction of wants. This alone promotes real happiness and contentment, and increases the capacity for service.[40]

Gandhi distinguished between a high standard of living and high standard of life—the former more appropriately called the complex way of living, promoting neither health nor beauty, freedom nor joy.[41] Bharatan Kumarappa, a Gandhian writer, reinforces this:

> A man whose needs are few such as can be met by himself can afford to raise his head high and refuse to bow to any power which seeks to enslave him. Not the man with a so-called high standard of living. Every new luxury he adopts becomes an additional fetter preventing him from freedom of thought, movement, and action.[42]

Gandhi inextricably tied societal service with inner development. "Satyagraha," truth-force (or soul force, as Martin Luther King called it), could not be a means for overcoming division, unless it represented in itself the active experience of the unity of life, of a love rooted beneath the surface of things. The work of the true servant of society is to reawaken from day to day that consciousness of unity and freedom in oneself and others, "preparing in interior silence and consecrated action a place for the future to be born."[43]

---

[40]Quoted in the article by Ralph Ellsberg, "Economics for Peace," in *The Catholic Worker*, Vol 42, #1 (Jan. 1976).

[41]*Ibid.*

[42]*Ibid.*

[43]*Ibid.* For further insight into Gandhi, read *All Men Are Brothers (A Gandhi Reader)* and *The Way of All the Earth* by John Dunne.

World Development

Such call to greater simplicity and union of personal and social development is particularly timely for us. We live in a nation that is fast gobbling up the world's limited natural resources, one that presses (and models for others) a growth economy to consume still more, and that disastrously confuses standard of living and standard of life. We are a nation (perhaps like all nations) where "enough" is always more," as Henry Atkins, a priest friend of mind, often puts it. Governor Jerry Brown of California once said in the face of enormous demands for a share of the state budget: "There aren't enough cookies in the jar to meet everyone's demands." That gives us two basic possible directions in the years ahead:

1. Increased violence, exhausted resources, injustice, division, bitterness, larger military and police forces to protect what we pile up, and more public debt for our children to bear, as we continue to grab for all we can, at all cost, in a situation of growing world material scarcity and space.

2. Increased hope for mutual trust, husbanded and shared resources, and reduced fear if we advocate a simpler and more qualitative standard of life for all, resist confusion of this life with material standard of living, and press for economic structures that support this simplicity.

Obscuring The Holy

We cannot control which choice will be made by others, but we can influence our own toward the second. "Looseness" is a good first step: looseness toward "having," toward identifying ourselves with what we "have" rather than with what we "are": bearers of the divine image. That image cannot be "added to" by our tightly held possessions, only obscured.

It is easier for a camel to go through the eye of a needle than for a rich man to enter the kingdom of God (Mt.19:24).

Fool! This night your soul is required of you; and the things you have prepared, whose will they be? So is he who lays up treasure for himself, and is not rich toward God (Lk. 12:21).

Americans

Most Americans are rich by the standards of Jesus' day. We know its emptiness, its surface comfort, its false promise, its diversionary power. Realizing this through our personal and national experience, perhaps our greatest prophetic task is to act on this truth. We can press for a reduction of over-production and over-consumption. We can shift that primary energy into ways of evoking and celebrating the shared divine image in us, rather than into ways of making ever more money off of each other. Such service will involve assuring a basic standard of material living for all: shelter, health care, food, clothing, and educational opportunity. But our service presses on beyond these, into that moment of emptiness when the survival struggle ceases and one asks, "Now what?" That is a religious question whose answer has political consequences.

Prophetic Simplicity

Simplicity in prophecy is important. If we take it with heavy seriousness, then our egos easily become attached: "I" am going to "show" the world what is right. "We" are going to "save" the world. Then we tend to become very self-important, cold, rigid, and lacking in that light openness to grace which reminds us of the ever-surprising mystery of life in God's hands.

Simplicity in prophecy means almost casually doing whatever we decide to do about our life style and social actions. Make no big deal out of it. Expect no one to "follow." Judge no one for not following. Just do what you feel called to do after testing your sense of calling with those you trust. The result may be that no one "hears" your prophecy except you yourself at the moment. Accept that as sufficient. If others join you (or you them), fine. Let it be a pilgrimage, not a grand battle plan with the conclusion already written in your mind. Move one step at a time. Be patiently attentive for the next step to reveal itself. Look ahead with hope, and with what planning is called for,[44] but mainly keep yourself open

[44]And this can be very careful planning; the simplicity I am suggesting is not an excuse to ignore the data we need to have at hand for responsible decision-making, and the hard work it can take to get this data.

and present, here now. Then social pilgrimage simply con·
tinues personal pilgrimage, and vice versa. There is no complicating split.

Frustration

So many times we become frustrated in our serving:
"Why doesn't she stop killing herself with drugs?" "Why
doesn't he ever see the point?" "That person just sulks and
sulks and never grows up." "No one ever thanks me."
"What's the use? He just goes out and gets drunk again."
"She's squandering her health and energy." "He refuses to
face up to his irresponsible life." "That city council is so
corrupt; it's hopeless." "That community association I
helped form now is trying to keep out poor people."

Expectations

Frustration comes from expectations. Compassionate
serving at its best is free of tight expectations. We just do
what we are moved to do. We can be aware of the possible
consequences and have particular hopes, but these need a
certain lightness. A gift is a gift is a gift. Throw it on the
waters and let the current bring it where it will. If it is not
inspired by the Holy Spirit, then it will dissolve. If it is, then
the current must finally nourish the gift and bring it Home.

*My word shall not return to me empty, but it shall ac-
complish that which I purpose (Is. 55:11).*

Chapter Eight: Eating

The disciples besought him, saying, "Rabbi, eat." But he said to them, "I have food to eat of which you do not know." So the disciples said to one another, "Has any one brought him food?" Jesus said to them, "My food is to do the will of him who sent me and to accomplish his work" (Jn.4:31-34).

How we eat is a telltale barometer of our sense of life at the moment. Sometimes we feel a gnawing emptiness or anxiety inside. We "locate" that feeling in our stomachs, and we feel ravenously hungry. But the hunger is for security, for love, for acceptance. We stuff ourselves at the table, and, for a while, we are filled. We can "buy" such substitute fulfillment with food. We can make it care for us, just as we can buy a prostitute's or gigolo's caresses.

A Gift

When we are at peace in our sense of purpose and being loved, in that moment eating takes on a different quality. It becomes much less compulsive, much more optional, needed only for the body's nourishment. If that peace rises from the bottom of the well in us, from a place so deep and spacious that we sense its indestructibility, its sheer givenness, then food takes on subtler qualities than bodily feeding. It becomes a delightful gift expressing the mysterious Giver's love. And it becomes a natural opportunity for sharing that love.

Such sacramental quality easily is blurred in the way food comes to us day by day: the impersonal mass packaging of a supermarket, the rush of a fast food carry-out, the clanging of the food chain's cash register, signaling its profit-making focus.

Food's subtle quality also can be lost in the midst of an angry family table, or one where meals are staggered by different family member schedules or indifference, so that no one eats together.

The sacrament also is stillborn when the food is a half-noted sideshow before the TV set or newspaper.

In such ways we dull our senses and miss the great window into life that eating can be.

Scripture

Food is woven through the Bible, as it is through the day. It crops up rhythmically, book by book, as a sign of divine caring and chastisement, and of human sharing. The New Testament gives special attention to eating as a divine window: it is the way through which God is revealed—in bread and wine, in loaves and fishes, in eating with tax collectors and sinners and a just-married couple. This revelation also happens in reverse attentiveness: abstaining from food, fasting. Again and again eating (or abstaining) is a sign pointing to a heavenly banquet, to a deeper human purpose and power, to a spring of water that forever quenches our thirst.

How can we allow eating to reveal such radiant secrets hidden just beneath its surface?

Growing

We can begin by growing some food for ourselves. Even if you live in an apartment, you at least can grow herbs, like parsley and mint, which can be picked and used to flavor and decorate many dishes. Growing food gets you into it from the very beginning: planting and watering a dead-looking seed or tiny plant, watching it grow into maturity, picking this little miracle and using it to nourish our bodies. Such a process allows us to be in that amazing cycle of life. In sudden flashes, in the midst of watering or spading, when we are simply present, the plant becomes a window through which we see life for the gift it is. We see ourselves in that gift: not mechanically "made," but wondrously grown; not all blueprinted and constructed, but unfolding into an ever more unique, never-before expression of life's holy seed.

Cooking

Everyone can learn how to cook. This experience can be shared by all the members of a household. It is too precious a window to be restricted to one person's privilege. Our capacity to shape and transform raw ingredients into a balanced meal of beauty and taste reveals that marvelous power of creativity that expresses our divine image in the simplest, most practical way. Perhaps this awareness was present subconsciously in that rich banker in Boston I once heard about who, at the age of fifty, chucked his lucrative and prestigious job to become a small restaurant cook, and claimed a vocational happiness he had never known. Cooking for others as well as ourselves, and eating with others: these are most direct and delightful ways to share life.

Cooking need not be elaborate. The simplest ingredients and recipes can make the finest meals. If we keep the menu simple, perhaps then we can afford to shop at smaller stores more often, where we can buy really fresh vegetables and natural, processed grains for bread, cereal, rice and beans (and also where we might have a little more personal relation with the grocer).

While cooking, let yourself be simply present in what you're doing, so present that you are fully satisfied with each moment, sensing the Kingdom as much in the midst of this act as in the midst of any other. Give yourself enough time so you needn't "rush" it. Rushing tightens you up, forces you ahead of yourself, and out of simple presence.

Fasting

We can fast, either in a partial form—abstinence from killed animals, for example—or temporarily from all food. Voluntary fasting is a special kind of attentiveness to food, and to our hungry neighbors.

Fasting is not easy in a nation where TV ads, billboards, endless strings of food stores, restaurants, and food machines entice us to eat and drink wherever we turn. It is made more difficult by the down-playing of fasting by the churches in recent years (though the focus on world hunger today has stimulated a mini-revival). The only power fasting seems to maintain is in the doctor's mouth when s/he tells us we've been eating too much and it's ruining our health!

Yet fasting can be enormously instructive and beneficial: to ourselves, as well as to others through the food we save and example we set.

The body seems to naturally fast when we are sick; it knows that the first cells eaten when no new food comes are the old and sick cells. Fasting literally cleanses the body of unneeded and "complicating" cells.

Fasting also can simplify the compulsive, distracting, grasping nature of our appetites. When we fast intentionally, one of the first things we notice is how little food we really need, yet how much we have been wolfing down. The dull, bloated feeling from over-eating slowly vanishes. We become lighter and more lucid. We see that we really are capable of not responding to that grasping wave of appetite that clicks in our brain. That is a little realization of freedom. If we don't respond to that shallow, driving wave, we are free to flow in a simpler, deeper, more even-flowing stream.

This freedom can have a multiplier effect on our other

appetites. We find that we need respond less to other waves of aggressive, grasping desire that shoot up. We become more and more simply present, able to see more clearly the concrete situation we are in, and care more gently and concertedly for it.

My own and others' experience leads me to recommend not a full fast, but a "juice fast": vegetable juice (preferably freshly made) and especially fruit juice (which will provide more energy sugar) three times a day. The juice provides a basic, simple, appropriate nourishment. It can save you from the complicating distractions of headaches and hunger pangs that more easily accompany total fasting. Take plenty of water in addition to the juice throughout the day to prevent dehydration.

If you want to undertake a fast, it is easiest to do so with others. You can do this, for example, during a weekend corporate retreat, or as a family during traditional fast days. When all fast together, it not only reinforces our sense of capacity for it, but it frees us a bit from the temptation to see what we are doing as something very "special." Such fantasies are "extra"—more than the act calls for.

Fasting, finally, is ordinary, very human, simple, and found in virtually every religious tradition the world has known. Mindless gorging of ourselves is much more the abnormal, complicating, self-defeating way.

Attention

We can eat more attentively. This happens naturally when we are undergoing a partial fast. We tend to pay attention to food in a new way—to be less "mindless" about it. When you have only a glass of juice in front of you, the mechanical operation of eating is very simple, and the mind is free to see what otherwise may be crowded out.

Here are five specific disciplines of attentiveness drawn from many wells of spiritual tradition. They are most effective if you are eating in silence: alone or with others.[45] But they are possible "in the cracks" of a talking meal, as well.

1. With a deep sense of thanksgiving let your mind trace back all the things you can think of involved in getting that food to you: the seeds, earth, rain, sun, plant, tree, pickers, movers, packagers, grocers, etc.

You can continue seeing this life cycle by sensing the food becoming nutrients for your body, excrement, returning to the earth, and the whole cycle beginning again. Accept this ever changing flow as integral to life: see that there is nothing you need hold onto, not even yourself. God's blessing is in this process.

2. Let yourself see the many hungry persons in the world, near and far. Let this strengthen your careful selection of food to eat, your prayer for those people and your simple, non-violent resolve to work for the better distribution and

[45]Eating in silence as a family or community once in a while can be quite refreshing. I know one parent who claimed that his children became far less "grasping for more" and happily calm during occasional silent meals (I assume the parents became that way, too!). Music can be used as a backdrop, or

quality of the planet's resources in whatever way is given you. Let yourself sense the preciousness of this little bit of food for life.

3. Set an extra place at the table. Focus on it in silence. Serve that place just as you are served. Flash people into that place as you eat: people you know, don't know, in this country and others, rich, poor, saint, sinner, everyone. They all are there. Maintain a simple sense of sharing throughout the meal. See how your eating continues your serving of life. Be open to the opportunity of filling that vacant place at the table with someone in need.

4. Stay silently aware in every moment of the process of eating a bite of food (or drinking a sip of juice or other liquid). Be mindful of all the processes involved, so that each is done attentively: the intention to look at the food; turning toward it; seeing consciousness of its color rise, then of the food itself; intention to move your hand to take the food; moving your hand; touching the food or glass; intention to lift your arm (with no sense of "me" or "mine"); lifting your arm; intention to open your mouth; opening; intending to put the food in your mouth; putting; the sensation of the food on the tongue; intention to close your mouth; closing; intention to put your arm down; doing it; intending to chew (if it is solid food); chewing; taste coming and disappearing; intention to swallow; swallowing. Do not reach immediately for more; gently check the greed for

someone reading out loud (as in the classic monastic tradition), or everyone can focus on one of the forms of attentiveness mentioned here. A blessing said or sung at the beginning of the meal can be the last words heard until the meal is over.

more taste sensation. Repeat this process with each bite or drink (if it is a silent meal).

Doing this becomes a simple, mindful, flowing, ungrasping presence in the process. Our mind is not wandering somewhere else, doing "extra" things. It is not heedlessly shoveling down "stuff." It is full attentiveness in present experience, wherein simplicity resides.

5. If you are trying to fast in some form and having a great deal of trouble letting go your appetite, you can take the extreme step of meditating on food as something repulsive. The dirt and excrement in root crops; the chemicals used to preserve food; the tongue turning it over, mixed with spit at the end of the tongue, a nauseating mixture like dog's vomit; swallowing and dropping it into a ( ) year old stinking, unwashed bag (your stomach). With meat you can be even more vivid!

When we find ourselves eating mindlessly, it just complicates it the more to add judgment. Instead, just notice what you are doing, gently smile, and so subtly loosen your bonds to inattentive appetite. Great feast days, of course, are exceptions! The very meaning of a feast is an overflowing participation/celebration set off from the day-to-day routine. But even then, know what you are doing. Know that the stuffing, finally, is optional. You don't need it, but you can have it. You can choose freely to partake or not. You can be master, not slave, to appetite.

Eating is one of those gnawing passions of the body you need not attach yourself to, either with rejection or affirmation. It is just there. You can lightly play with it, you can enjoy it, you can share it, you can allow eating to be a window to life's secrets. But if you grasp it tightly or dully, the window shade snaps shut, and the joy and sharing are missed. It is no accident that fasting is such a universal spiritual discipline. It is one of the first acts of simplification that frees us for others, and for our own deeper awareness.

Chapter Nine: Playing

Do not be anxious for your life; your Father cares . . . .
Seek first his Kingdom–and all these things shall be yours
as well (Mt. 6:25, 33).

A Problem

Following a talk on "vacations" at a parish church recently, an elderly man came up and told me the sad story of the people in his business office. One of his close friends was about to retire. He looked ahead to that moment with terror. His life had been spent driving, pushing, getting ahead, and staying ahead. He didn't have a clue what it meant not to work.

The man then told me: "There's nothing you can do for him. It's too late. But I fervently hope we can help those people who have just reached forty"—those men and women who have reached a point of questioning how much time they are putting into their work, who would like to have a more balanced rhythm of the day.

Then a forlorn look came over his face as he said:

But, you know, if you slacken up a little, you can't even stay where you are. Others will climb right on over you. You'll find yourself further and further down the ladder!

There we have a problem! Both an inside and an outside problem. And there will be no real playing until we've coped with it.

The outside problem is the most obvious. Hard work has

built and enriched the nation's (and sometimes the world's) well-being enormously. But too much of it raises the old saw: "All work and no play makes Jack a dull boy!" The dullness is living with a badly faded memory of what life is all about. Grinding away day by day wears such a deep groove into us that our needles get stuck in it; we find ourselves just going round and round. We've lost the point. We just do it in a kind of stupor.

Work

A powerful segment of society can get lost this way together. The norms of organizations get set up to reinforce hard, endless work. The motive and reward of material profit and status is there, and sometimes other motives: service, creativity, fellowship. But even these can fade, and there we are day by day going together from rushed breakfast to job to a short collapse at home to work again. We burn ourselves up. We burn up the world's energy and goods. We relentlessly consume ourselves and nature.

For some such work is a tragic necessity for survival (or, worse, not available at all). But for many there is more: If we don't do all that, others will do it and get ahead. We will lose merits. We won't keep up. Or belong. Or get the things we want. Or help a good reputation for the next job referral. Or keep the world going. At least such things are what we say if people ask. But what would we do if we didn't work hard? Could I really stand more free time?

Making It Happen

That's the *internal* problem. Even if the external environment is set up for us *not* to work so much, we tend to work hard at playing—which then really is just work in disguise. The magical quality of work is its illusion that we really can control life that way. Working is making something happen. If we just work hard enough, we can make things come out the way we want. Then life becomes more efficient, free of messiness, safe, predictable—maybe someday even immortal.

Work is good. But it promises too much. Towers of Babel are work. They can be beautiful and helpful. But they don't reach heaven. If that's what we secretly hope, we're bound for disappointment. Towers reach only ever emptier and more lonely sky. The gates of heaven cannot be stormed.

A Window

So what can we do? Work to serve and create and survive. But let's not confuse it with salvation. That, ultimately, is given. At best our work—whatever it is—forms another window for us to look through, just as our eating, serving, and relating.

Don't be anxious about what things you will get. First be attentive to heaven-in-your-midst. The rest will be given, as you have need.[46]

A foretaste of heaven in the midst of work can come through

---

[46]A loose paraphrase of Jesus in Mt. 6:25, 33.

a kind of surprising playfulness. In the very midst of our work a sparkling edge, a glimmer of spaciousness some times shines through. Our workmate, with whom we have various tensions, suddenly appears incredibly lovable and totally acceptable. While reading an article for work (even the Bible!) a sentence or misprint suddenly lights a smile in us. The silverware all tangled up in the sink take on a ludi-rous, marvelous shape. These moments slacken the taut-ness of our work rope. Something slips through that allows us fresh presence: a tiny taste of something more than our crowded efforts.

That presence always is light and spacious, and often funny. If you think about real humor a minute, you see how it is a kind of explosion inside that blows open a little hole in our tightness; sometimes it clears away a lot of clinging debris clogging us up and weighing us down.

In our work then we can be attentive for this sparkle that nudges us from over-attachment to what we are doing. That invites us to a moment of divine play It's the angel on your shoulder doing the nudging—enjoy it!

Then there is our "organized" playing. Sports, vacations, TV, music, hobbies, and liturgies.[47] How can we save these from work? How can we let organized play be a window, too? Allowing it to be one more overlay on life, through which we can be simply present on heaven's sparkling edge?

Let's take two arenas of play for special attention: sports and vacations.

[47]Yes, liturgies. What are they at heart but end-in-themselves celebrations of life's gift?

Spectator Sports

"Sports," declares Michael Murphy,[48] "is America's yoga." It is our primary way of organized, disciplined, playful attentiveness through our bodies (and created extensions of our bodies: bats, balls, clubs, racquets, gloves, uniforms, shoes).

For millions of people sports is largely a vicarious experience: watching others from our seats. This is a special boon to handicapped and older people. And perhaps a bane for many others when watching becomes an excuse for shunning direct, first-hand participation. I used to despise "spectator sports." I wanted to get in there and really be a part.

Spectatorship felt like reading the great mystics of the Church describe their experiences. That was fascinating. And there was a little secret sigh of relief at the safe distance I was from all that awesome, purging, first-hand involvement. But deep down I knew that satisfaction with mere observation of others' experience was cheating my basic human nature, which yearned for its own unique, first-hand knowledge. Soren Kierkegaard[49] once said, in effect, that admiration is a cop-out. If we really are impressed with someone's courage or holiness, then that's a signal to "do thou likewise."

I've grown to appreciate "spectatorship" a little more now. For one thing, I'm old enough to know that I never will be courageous or skillful or holy in the way that other people are. This isn't a personal "put-down." Each of us is

[48]Founder of The Esalen Institute in California.

[49]A great nineteenth-century Danish theologian

gifted and capable of a unique expression of the divine image in us. Nobody can be a better me than me, or a better you than you. But I know there are some gifts that others have and I don't, so why not enjoy them from the stadium or in front of the television set?

I've also discovered an edge of holy sanity in the madness of competitive sports. When I have a team to support, then I seem more capable of really getting involved, energized, alert, present. The danger, of course, is over-attachment to the team! But when I identify just enough, then there is a kind of primitive simple presence possible, a vibrant attentiveness that sloshes out the dullness inside. I'm not expecting the heavens to open as a spectator—but they're not tightly locked out then, either, as I once believed.

Participative Sports

A clear opportunity for meditation, for simple presence, for a playful window, can be found in participative sports. The yoga postures mentioned earlier invite simplicity. Simplicity takes more attentiveness in sports, where we have to cut through achievement syndroms and complex-looking techniques.

These are cut to a minimum in a sport like fishing, at least if we don't get fancy and just throw a line out and watch the cork! Millions of fishermen are playfully meditating all the time. That cork bobbing around patiently for hours has been a window into many a holy place—though often forgotten and ineffective, I'm afraid, because no one expects fishing to be a holy window.

Books are coming out now that treat such sports as golf, jogging, and tennis as means of simple attentiveness. I have also heard of skiing being taught in this way, and even scuba diving. These are signs of a much more holistic view of sports emerging today: the "I've got to make the varsity team" is beginning to be challenged by "I'm just going to do this sport as a mantra, a backdrop for my simple, flowing presence in life."

I have played tennis for twenty-five years. For a long time I've had a dim awareness that it wasn't just a game I was playing. I have come to sense that it is really *less* than a game, at its best: it's just being there fully present is the rhythm of the bouncing ball. The more present I am, the less self-conscious I become: the less of an observer, commentator, judge, competitor. A quality of subjective presence comes. Everything just "happens." It's all together—a playing out of the way life is at bottom.

I'm far more aware now of my distorted views of life at other moments during the game: when I feel that I "have" to win, or lose confidence and feel "I'm no good" (then proving it by missing the ball!), or when I feel that I must please the other person, or that I can "make" it all come out right if I just play a little harder and more carefully. I sense such feelings in others too, now. In fact, watching a person play is like seeing a projection of his or her view of life. We are all very naked on a tennis court: our attitudes and behavior there weave a picture of who we are more vividly than any psychological or spiritual write-up possibly could.

Awareness that tennis (as well as many other sports) reveals much of the way we see and live life is one discovery of simplicity. When we play, we haven't entered some other bounded category, some other fragment of life unconnected with the others. Play is just another overlay through which who we are all the time is revealed, and through which we can see the same life that's always there in a fresh way. Child psychologists long ago learned that watching children at play can tell them a great deal about the way children see life. We never really outgrow that transparency in play.

Learning a sport often is taught as an enormously complicated and technical affair. The emerging "contemplative" approach allows much greater beauty and simplicity—and continuity with other arenas for spiritual awareness.

Listen to Tim Gallway describe the process of learning as I heard him describe it on one of his Public Broadcasting Corporation TV programs ("The Inner Game of Tennis"[50]):

If you are relaxed, alert, and interested, then you can't help but learn . . . Learning is natural, organic . . . like the

[50]Refer also to his book by that title.

194

way a child learns to walk: without judgment or comparison.

In Gallway's teaching he emphasizes making friends with the ball, loving it, intently focusing on its seams. He asks that you allow your mind to be even and present, not trying to force your body to do something, but letting your body move in its own balanced wisdom.

Archery as a similar means of attentive presence in Zen Buddhist tradition was described twenty years ago by a Westerner, Eugene Herrigel.[51] Perhaps now we are moving toward a fresh meeting ground for mutual East-West enrichment. Sports in any case need never again be perceived as some complicated "other" category of life. They are a bodily art form, a two-way mirror that reflects how we see life, and can reveal how it really is.

Vacations

God rested on the seventh day, but we're never told what he really did. We've been fumbling around with rest time ever since. Usually we treat the other six days as the really important time, in the same way that we often treat active, busy prayer as more important than quiet prayer. In work time we know what to do. But what about when there's nothing we have to do? That leaves an edge of "vacant"— "empty" time, an edge of anticipation, and yet an edgy edge of anxiety and even panic. If we don't turn it into a time for

[51]Zen in the Art of Archery (Pantheor. 1953).

more crowded work, then we're tempted to treat it as time to kill: with sleep, drink, dull staring at the tube, empty talk, walking around in a kind of dazed stupor—waiting for the busy womb of the work day to swallow us up again.

The British still keep the old English word for rest days: "holiday." The don't do any better with them than we do, but their fondness for historic preservation at least keeps the skeletal word alive from a time when rest time was holy time, holy day. Accounts of medieval holy days show some unholy edges, but nonetheless there was a sense of full, playful, and shared celebration that assumed an underlying value to rest time: a special window into that divine radiance just beneath the workaday surface.

In the balanced day and week such rest time is always there: in prayer, in gathering with others for sheer enjoy ment, in sports, in reading a good novel.

In a balanced year, that rest time needs extension into larger chunks of time: a week here, two weeks there, or maybe a month. A real vacation. In retirement, of course, this chunk can take up the whole year.

When we plan for that time, our situations at different moments in our lives leave open many different pos- sibilities. Sometimes we plan, control, and package it so thoroughly that it's finished before beginning, dead before having a chance to live. There's that little devil in us who sees to it that we make sure nothing new has a chance to get through to us. Then we become mere tc urists on vacation:

looking dully from the outside; seeing nothing but what neatly fits into, reinforces, and entertains our closed view of life. We trek through a pre-determined scene, buying slides of it made long before we arrived.

Returning from such a vacation we find that devil inside us relieved and happy: we made it through that potentially unpredictable time without a scratch. We're back just as we left. No window flew open filled with a view of God-knows-what-unsettling-thing. Keeping that window closed was tense and complicated. But we did it. And we're home safe.

But some place deeper inside we feel a little empty and cheated. We never really trusted enough to let the window open and join that playful divine dance always beckoning between the cracks of our crowded minds: especially during the great crack vacation allows.

Another common medieval experience besides the single holy day was the pilgrimage. When a person had more time than a single holiday, a frequent way of stretching it out was by making a pilgrimage. I find much inspiration in the image of pilgrim as an option to tourist. Anagarika Govinda, a German-born Buddhist lama now a very old man in this country, describes the meaning of pilgrimage in the process of writing about his own to Tibet:[52]

A "pilgrimage" distinguishes itself from an ordinary journey by the fact that it does not follow a laid-out plan or

[52]Anagarika Govinda, *The Way of the White Clouds* (Shamhala, 1966).

198

itinerary, that it does not pursue a fixed aim, or a limited purpose, but that it carries its meaning in itself, by relying on an inner urge which operates on two planes, physical and spiritual. It is a movement not only in the outer, but equally in the inner space, a movement whose spontaneity is that of the nature of all life, i.e., of all that grows continually beyond its momentary form, a movement that always starts from an invisible inner core.

Each of us can choose to approach vacation time as an open pilgrimage, rather than a closed tourist trap. We can plan out the time roughly: where we're going, whom we will see, what we will do. But inwardly we know this is just an expedient structure, a kind of network of activity where our sight will be on the little open spaces between the netting On pilgrimage we are waiting on God, for what we do not know, yet which we trust enough to keep an open door. Through all we see and do and feel, there is a kind of presence maintained beneath the surface, an open space where we maintain an even mind, but a gently expectant one, willing to be caught up and pulled into the freshness of divine play.

This may not happen. We cannot demand it. We can't *make* someone play with us! We may be on pilgrimage for years before we're ready for such grace. But open attentiveness invites divine play. Certainly it will be more likely then than with "tourist" mind. And when it happens, then the whole year, not only vacation, is opened to pilgrimage.

When we trust that salvation cannot be earned, but that
    we can allow space for its realization—
When we trust that life is basically confident and grace-
    ful at its Heart—
Then we are free to play,
And not bound by the twin labors of crowded work and
    empty escape.

Chapter Ten: Aching

A thorn was given me in the flesh . . . but he said to me, "My grace is sufficent for you, for my power is made perfect in weakness" (2 Cor. 12:7, 9).

Allowing

Until God becomes "all in all," everything in life has its aching side. If we become lost in this side of things, we sink into depression. If we warp aching into pleasure, we ask to be hurt, or enjoy hurting others.

Aching is very powerful. It has a way of crowding out everything else in our consciousness:

An aching body . . .

Aching heart . . .

Aching neighbor .

Aching neighborhood.

Endless unfulfilled desires and uninvited pains.

But if we allow aching to teach us, and bear it in trust, then we can come through to its other side. There, even if the ache remains, it is more light, spacious, free, and wise. There the sun shines through it; the ache is shaken off center stage to the shadowy fringe.

Lightening

Let's look a little closer at the aching now and see if there aren't some ways we can lighten its heavy, complicated, dominating side, leaving room for its open side to appear.

I never cease being shocked at the first impact of sickness and injury. On my way home from the office recently I suddenly became aware that a different disposition had taken me over: where a few minutes before I was alert, energetic, cool, now I was listless, tired, and hot. When I arrived home, the usual joy at seeing my children run up to me and talk about their day now was replaced by a bare tolerance, an annoyance at their loudness, a general lack of appreciation or participation in the life around me. No dinner, please. Just leave me alone. I'm going to bed.

That was the beginning of my last bout with the flu. My clarity was gone. Everything of value seemed soured and suspended. I felt like a passive pawn in the grip of this virus.

Our body aches may be much more serious and land us in the hospital. Or they may be steady "thorns in the flesh": backaches, dizziness, arthritis, headaches, the loss of a limb, failing eyesight or hearing, or the unsteadiness of old age. Perhaps the aching isn't in the outer body but in the inner heart: from the loss of a loved one or of a job, or the constant fear of crime around us, or loneliness for a close friend, or some injustice suffered or seen.

So what can we do?

Drugs

We can drug ourselves. American medicine is extremely sophisticated in ways of killing pain, well beyond the old glass of whiskey. But it is unfortunately not very good at not killing our clear awareness along with it. "Don't drive a car while under the influence of this pill." Why? Because we're not quite in touch with reality any more. We're kind of high and floating around a bit—not quite "all there." And then there are all the other side-effects that no one is quite sure about.

In our heavily drugged culture there is a kind of tacit assumption that pain is a natural enemy, of no possible value, to be killed at all costs. Maybe we need to be a little more discriminating about this. Sometimes it's true. But sometimes it's not. Our bodies, after all, don't "want" to ache. They ache because something's wrong. The aching is telling us something. Doctor after doctor has told me that a great many patients come to them with complaints that are symptoms of more subtle mental and spiritual aches (which they usually are not equipped to handle). All the drugs do then is kill the voice of illness. We don't stay with the pain long enough to "hear" that deeper, more threatening ache that says we need to face into life somewhere that we're not. Or perhaps we know the deeper ache, but despair of anything that can be done about it.

Talking With a Confidant

If we sense a deeper voice behind our aching, then we had better go easy on the drugs and heavy on talking with a confidant who might help us evoke that hidden "complication," or help us gain new courage to find a way through one we already are clear about.

We can be very hesitant about unraveling such problems

with friends (or therapists or clergy). We need the courage of humility on the one hand; willingness to let someone else in on our specific ways of sharing human frailty. That's kind of a comedown from the more vaunted self-image we often like to maintain. The higher we are in community status, the harder it can be for us to remember that the same pall[53] hangs over all caskets for a reason: because there is no more than a hair's breadth between us in holiness and frailty.

On the other hand we need confidence that we have a right to go to another and they have a concern to listen. Endless biblical passages about bearing one another's burdens and suffering together invite us toward that confidence.

The simpler we manage to go about this, the better. It need not be a long, drawn-out struggle: "Will I ask to talk with so-and-so or won't I?" "What will happen?" "What will s/he think of me?" Carrying on that inner debate too long can lead to over-concern, over self-importance even. Just do it! Asking another human being for help after all is an ancient, well-tested, natural, soul-nourishing means of grace.

Be Simplified

We can let the ache be simplified to its basic energy, and go "behind" or "into" it. This is not easy. Much energetic concentration and practice is needed. But, when successful,

---

[53]A pall is a white or purple "blanket" that is placed over the casket during a burial service in some Christian traditions, symbolizing the equality of everyone before God at death.

we are not quite such passive pawns in the hands of the pain. Bio-feedback methods try to do this with machines. It is possible without them.

a. Note the pain, and then gently, in a flash, move "behind" it with your mind to its "other side"; stay there in that expansive, open space as long as you can (but with no sense of "forcing" it). Pain always has this clear "other side."

b. Move your mind into the "center" of the pain with great (but relaxed) concentration. Do this so completely that there is no sense of anyone left to have the pain. You can experience a kind of transmutation of energy (as in "a" above), which opens your mind rather than constricts it. In a sense then you are veering the energy of pain away from its complicating problems, toward a quality of expansive simplicity.

Reading

We can read, or have someone read to us, stories and passages that show understanding of pain, both its heavy and light side.

Many psalms are fine reading at such times. There is a bald honesty in them that goes through every possible mental convolution: anger at God, despair, tears, condemnation of other people, bargaining with God, hope, pleading, shock, remembrance of past deliverance, rejoicing, thanksgiving.

Four good ones at such times are Psalms 42, 91, 103 and 130. Where "enemies" are mentioned, my mind sometimes reads "viruses," "bacteria," "shoddy cars that cause accidents," etc. This is tricky, though. In one sense these are enemies calling for resistance, but they can disguise angelic visitors trying to tell us something. So along with resistance, I see the need to keep my ears open for whatever grace may be revealed.

Reading the Gospel according to St. Luke, with all its many stories of sickness and healing, also can be helpful. Let yourself identify with the sick wanting to get well (not all sick people want to get well), and with Jesus coming to you as to them.

If you're feeling particularly bitter, despairing, or angry, then the Book of Job might be a good companion for your misery and help you get through it.

Prayer

We can pray. Alone or with others. The kinds of Scriptural passages just mentioned stimulate boldness in our own prayer. Allow great, confident, insistent energy to flow in your prayer; sense your openness for healing opening into the Healing One. Let your whole body be caught up in this openness. If some other faithful persons are near, ask them to prayerfully lay hands on you as an open channel of healing.

Give thanks for the grace there beyond our control or understanding. Grace isn't the same as healing. We want healing. We hope and pray for it. But grace is beyond healing. Grace is always there, simply present, through everything, whether or not it takes the form of that healing we want.

We can pray for others in the midst of our own pain. There's no time when we can identify better with the aches of others. Allowing concern and energy to flow toward them is most natural now. Such prayer has a way of saving us from centering life on our private pain. It opens us to the shared pain all around us.

I remember crying alone some months ago. I don't cry often, but something had happened in my life that just broke me down for a moment. In the middle of my heartache, I somehow found myself moving out in prayer for all the suffering of the world. An overwhelming feeling of belonging to that suffering side of all sentient beings came over me. In lifting my arms in prayer for myself, it seemed to become one inclusive intercession for the relief of all suffering, as though no one's could be ended finally unless everyone's was. The prayer then simply became a plea for the Kingdom to come, that fullness of the Kingdom of heaven when God "will wipe away every tear," and there shall be no more mourning nor crying nor pain.[54]

When life is going well, and my body is free from pain, I'm glad. But when that's too consistent, I notice a little more callousness and evasion inside me toward suffering. Though I hate aching, I recognize that tinge of grace in it that brings me closer to the suffering side of everyone, and

[54]Rev. 21:4.

opens up a little more compassion. Aching has a way of bringing us together. It also brings us deeper: frivolous and petty things fall away. We're a little closer to the nitty-gritty, to the hard side of life, and all the ways we escape or face into it (why else would we pay money to see tragic plays and films?).

My faith—what I really trust, or don't—I find exposed and tested during pain. When I face into it, I sense the truth of St. Paul's experience that suffering produces endurance and character and hope; that grace is made perfect in weakness.[55] I understand a little more intimately why the cross is such a powerful symbol, why Jesus can be so close to us. And I see how we cannot get to the resurrected side of life without going through its painful side.

Why? That is a fathomless mystery. No religious tradition has satisfactorily "explained" suffering. Yet all see the grace-full side of it, its capacity to purge us of vanity, pretense, callousness, and arrogance. "Faced into" suffering leaves us simpler, a bit more shorn of these blinding immaturities. What really is important in life stands out more clearly.

Aching certainly is not good in itself. But it is there. It can catch too neat, sleepy lives unawares, and, if we are attentive, shock us awake, becoming an unwanted but real means of grace.

[55]Rom. 5:3-5; 2 Cor. 12:9.

Chapter Eleven: Sleeping

"He gives to His beloved in sleep" (Ps. 127:2).

Taken

Late at night when I go into my children's room to make sure they're covered, I find their beds littered with toys and books. Sometimes one of these is still clutched in one hand. It's as though they suddenly had been caught unawares and "taken" into sleep, right in the middle of something else they were doing.

Sleep creeps up on us like that. Our adult "toys" may be a book or TV or active prayer or busy thoughts about the finished day or tomorrow. But there, between thoughts, suddenly we're "gone."

Perhaps we approach sleep in this indirect way because it is a little frightening to go into directly. Voluntary sleep requires a confidence that life is cared for when our ego is asleep at the wheel. The more we believe that life is safe and real only when we're awake and guarding and acting, the harder it is for us to let go into sleep. We go through all kinds of complex tricks to "make" us sleep, but trust in it is missing, and it comes then only when we're caught off guard.

A Happening

Sleeping is like pilgrimage vacations and quiet prayer. None of these really happens except by trusting and letting them happen. All require a loosening and simplification of our driving egos. If this is happening in the rest of our daily life, then the benefits spill over into an easier sleep.

There is an interesting passage in Ecclesiastes[56] that goes:

Sweet is the sleep of a laborer, whether he eats a little or much; but the surfeit of the rich will not let him sleep.

If we see "richness" as a complicated life of accumulation and protection, and "labor" as a symbol of a simpler, less striving life, then we see these spilling over into sleep. Then complexity and simplicity are taken with us into that shift in consciousness, and appear in restless or peaceful nights, in troubled or peaceful dreams.

If our trust and looseness is there enough, and sleep comes voluntarily, we've cleared a major hurdle. But if we place no real value on sleep other than restoration of bodily energy, we are likely to "sleep right through our sleep" and miss a third of our lives.

Sleep is only for the surface ego. Beneath, all is awake. Exactly what happens during that time is a great mystery and the subject of endless research. But much of importance does happen, particularly in our dreams.

Dreaming

On my first directed retreat many years ago, the director told me not to worry if I fell asleep: "God can speak to you in your dreams just as well as any other place." Scripture is full of references to important dreams. They are a special win-

[56]Eccl. 5:12.

dow into what's happening in our lives, into our desires and fears, and sometimes into the future: where we are being led, and what we can do. More rarely they can be windows into life far beyond our own: prophecies and events that relate to other people, or to whole peoples, or even beyond.

Dreams speak to us through symbols deeper than our conscious language. What these mean only we can know. And that knowing may be too deep for words. Perhaps we don't even need to try hard to "figure them out" rationally. Rational over-analysis can be very complicated and fanciful, reduce the dream to less than it is, and take us away from a simple aware presence in it. Perhaps that attentive awareness is enough, with just the barest, unforced rational connections.

The dreams may be just a continuation of our ego's play: our desires and fears expressed in symbolic form. These might show us more clearly just what desires and fears are shaped in us, and how these are hidden or integrated in our lives. If there is an "ache" in the dream, then that is a warning signal: something is pressing us, complicating us, and it needs attention.

Once in a while the dream may be more than this. We may wake with a start. We sense a specialness about it that says a deeper voice than our own ego is speaking (though there can be a very thin and uncertain line between). This may be a warning or blessing or calling focused on ourselves alone, or ourselves with others, or others apart from us. Since such a dream is so powerful—and often ambiguous and laden with action implications, it is best to bring it to someone we trust. With him or her we can test the dream's possible significance before acting on it.

As with all else we do, maintaining an even-minded simple attentiveness can be the fulcrum of our activity in dreaming. Then no nightmare need be quite so terrifying, nor demand for action quite so compulsive. We see what happens, we're in what happens, but we're not quite of it completely. There is an edge of freedom and clarity both in the dream and afterward. We rest in an indestructible confidence that nothing can appear which does not have the Loving One on its far side.

"He gives to His beloved in sleep." There is no one else to give, except the energy personifications of our own ambitions and our consequent vulnerability to the lesser "powers and principalities" of the world. To a confident, even mind, though, all these eventually are seen through as the empty bubbles they are. Such a mind, like a sharp pinpoint of truth, pops them and sees their negative energy dissolve, just as the "Wicked Witch of the West" dissolved when Dorothy threw water on her in *The Wizard of Oz*.

Dream Attentiveness

Everyone dreams. But not everyone remembers what s/he dreams. If you want to be attentive to this dimension of your

214

life, here are a few simple suggestions:

1. Just before falling asleep, confidently tell yourself that you will remember your dreams when you awaken. Sense this intent sinking into your subconscious mind.

2. Keep a pen or pencil and paper next to your bed. *Immediately* upon waking, write down what you remember of the dream. Do this before your mind wanders into any kind of interpretation.

If you awaken from a dream during the night, grab the pencil in the dark and scribble down a few key phrases that will help you recall it later.

3. Save a few minutes in the morning to read over your dreams. Don't try to force youself to understand them. Just "sit" with them awhile. If some associations with your life (or the lives of others) spontaneously emerge, write these down in a journal. If nothing comes, fine. You may find a pattern emerging over a period of weeks or months. You may not. Your simple awareness in their on-going flow is enough. If you stay attentive and open, if there is something in them of importance for life, it will emerge in its own time and way—perhaps unexpectedly in the middle of some other activity during the day.

Our "daydreams" can be treated in the same way.

4. A more radical attentiveness found in Eastern "dream yoga" involves treating the whole twenty-four hours as a dream, as one continuing flow of consciousness. Along with this, just before falling asleep at night visualize in your

throat an almost closed water lily (or some other flower that "closes up" in its daily rhythm), light pink in color. In the middle of this almost closed lily is a dim light. Keep this image still as you fall asleep. It can help you remain aware during your dreams.

Dying

Our ego is a solitary place, and he who rejects suffering and defies death and refuses to give himself, but wants to retain his self, shuts himself out of that Unity of all things which is God ("If the grain of wheat does not die, it remains alone . . . ").[57]

Falling into death is our last great sleep. Just as voluntary sleep is easier for the person who is dying daily to any sense of self as separate empire, so is voluntary dying. But I don't think it ever is really "easy" for anyone. Easy is just a relative term with dying. "Your time will come someday," said Don Juan to Castaneda. This is the hardest fact of all to accept. The older we become, the more we really begin to believe it. That we keep the fact buried even then, though, is borne out when a doctor tells someone s/he has "one year to live," and we see how the fact always known strikes the person as though never known: we see the shock and panic.

As with sleep, we are tempted to just "fall into" death unawares, in the midst of something else. It is too threatening to face head on.

[57]Ernesto Cardenal, *To Live Is To Love, op. cit.*

American culture until very recently reinforced the threat. Old age and death rarely have a place of honor with us. The dying are shut away wherever possible. Burials are passed through efficiently and quickly. In the last few years, though, more people are paying attention. Books, sermons, talks, and classes on death and dying suddenly have sprouted and spread. Perhaps this fresh interest is spawned by cultural shock at discovering the limits of our power to control the world: our defeat in Vietnam, on-going energy, food, and political crises, the deadly side-effects of many attempts at technological control of life, a rediscovery of the vengeance of nature when its balance is not reverenced.

Like a middle-aged person slowly feeling the outer edge of his or her powers and life-span, American society is maturing. Death to our powers is inevitable somewhere ahead. A crisis of values erupts, and we ask together, "What's really worth living for in the limited time we have left?" And, "How do we prepare for our dying?"

In Washington, D.C. two Episcopal priests began a new national, interfaith association several years ago, the "St. Francis Burial Society."[58] It is a harbinger, I believe, of the new time we are entering, where death (and therefore life) can be taken a little more seriously, simply, and in broad spiritual context.

The Society provides consultation services on ways of planning for a simple burial, and also on ways of preparing ourselves, the dying and the families of the dying or de-

[58]The Revs. William Wendt and Robert Herzog. For further information, including ways of forming branch chapters, and training programs for those working with the terminally ill, write the Society at 3421 Center St. N.W. Washington, D.C. 20010.

ceased to be involved realistically, directly, and helpfully with the whole process.

The Society also makes plain wood caskets, an ancient symbol of simplicity and equality at death (ones you're not likely to find available at your local funeral home). Such a casket can be bought years before you expect to die, and used as a functional part of your furniture (table, cabinet, etc.). This may seem gruesome to some people, but you also can look at it as a way of getting used to the reality of death, and reminding yourself to pay attention to what's important in life, not wasting time on petty grumblings.

The Society even has a "make it youself" casket, where you are just given the parts to assemble. Making your own casket, or having it made by friends, is an old custom. Constructing it with your hands can be a kind of ritual through which you assist and affirm your acceptance of death, and its implications for sorting out what is really important in life.

The greatest freedom of all perhaps is our freedom from fear of death. The more we bury it in some hidden corner of our minds, the more subtly it eats away at our daily lives, panicking us into ever more crowded and desperate living. Such concrete, literal preparations as suggested above can help us see to the other side of that fear. Really getting to the other side of it, though, is a gift of faith—an open trust that the Holy One lives on its other side. "Behold, He who keeps

Israel will neither slumber nor sleep."[59] If that is reality for us, then we know that death loses its hardest edge. If we see in Jesus Christ's resurrection a sign of the indestructibility of the Holy One in us, then we can exalt with St. Paul and shout:

Death is swallowed up in victory, O death, where is thy victory? O death, where is thy sting?[60]

Death, like sleep, cleanses life of many accumulated toxins. We need it. The earth needs it. The Kingdom needs it. Death is terrible. But it is given. Death is that final earthly winnowing that separates the wheat from the chaff, the sins and illusions to be burned from the pure light that is saved. If that process is going on in us all the time, then death is but one more step of purgation.

Perhaps it is not the last purgation. We may have on-going personal opportunity for shedding more of our chaff and more deeply living into the Heart of the Holy One.

Whatever happens, we can trust that the personal, the "our," will be caught up in "the twinkling of an eye"[61] and transformed into God's energy in some form. That energy cannot be lost. And there is no energy that is not finally in God.

[59]Ps. 121:41.

[60]1 Cor. 15:54-55.

[61]1 Cor. 15:51.

Postscript: How Far In Do You Want To Go?

"And just how far would you like to go in?" "Not too far but just far enough so we can say that we've been there." (Bob Dylan)

Tourist Mind

Yes that's "tourist mind," my friend. Moving around the edges of the day watching from a safe distance, putting a toe in here and there. That's "safe mind": arranging and rearranging everything to stay the same, to keep me separate and thinking I'm in command (a most complicated task!). That's "dammed up mind": holding back the great flood of awareness, letting out just a trickle that finds a lazy course of least resistance through the valley.

Such mind, carried to stubborn, defiant, closed extremes, is sinful mind, which strangles our unique gift.

Sin makes equals of us all; it makes us look like prisoners wearing the same uniform. Contrariwise, every saint is different, because sanctity is the full realization of the human personality, a recovery of that aboriginal identity which all beings once had.[62]

Open Mind

If we are not satisfied with this way, if we "want to go in' to truth further, we can be open for simple mind. It does not begin with harsh judgment of tourist mind. Simple mind starts with smiling mind: what is there is there Befriending tourist mind, seeing it clearly, accepting it *totally*, yet not

---

[62]Ernesto Cardenal, *To Live Is To Love*, op cit , p. 42.

identifying with it: these drain tourist mind of its strength. Its imperial, grasping, scared content is emptied through the sieve of attentive acceptance. That leaves an empty left hand free to receive from the grace-filled right. That is pilgrim mind. Open mind. Innocent mind melting fallen mind. Simple presence that leaves no split mind.

Such is the simple way, but it is not a lazy way. Its fullness involves every ounce of our energy and commitment.

Seeking

A Buddhist story tells of someone coming to a spiritual master, asking for the way to enlightenment. The master took him to a lake and held his head under water for a long time. When he finally lets the aspirant up, gasping for breath, the master tells him: "You must want enlightenment as much as you just wanted air to live."

In St. Benedict's sixth-century Rule for monks, he says of those who knock at the monastery door:

> When anyone is newly come from the reformation of his life, let him not be granted an easy entrance. (Instead, if the newcomer) perseveres in his knocking and if it is seen after four or five days that he bears patiently the harsh treatment offered him and the difficulty of admission, and that he persists in his petition, then let entrance be granted him.

The Simple Way

Jesus invites us to come: "Seek and you will find, knock and it will be opened to you." "My way is easy (simple?) and my burden light." But He also says, "Enter by the narrow gate . . . for the gate is narrow and the way hard that leads to life, and those who find it are few."

The way of simplicity is open for everyone. But it requires "all" of us. Total attentiveness. If we play around with it, the result will be the same as with every game: when it's over, "real life" is the same. There is no transformation. The same dull suffering and delusion is still there.

And if we grasp for it hard? Then also we lose simple presence. Crude grasping only tightens the power of our fist. We cannot make the rose unfold by pulling open its petals. That will only destroy it. Our total energy rather needs to be there in the unfolding process, allowing it to happen, watering and fertilizing and watching patiently from within. Then at bottom we are neither passive nor active, but simply present.

So often I am far from that simple presence. Each day I play and strive and live out of tourist mind. Lingering within me is the illusion that I will be saved by piling up a little more knowledge, finding the right insight, the right book, the right guru, the right prayer, the right action. Sometimes I despair completely. But then I've learned to count that as progress.

Patient Unknowing

Not long ago I heard myself say to someone, "I know less now than I did a year ago." I have begun to despair of knowledge that needs despairing: knowledge that is grasping, deflecting, complicating, obscuring, misleading. There is a little more "unknowing" in me. That means an opening—an open hole in the middle where I can be present more freshly in the unique moment. But how quickly the hole closes as the grasping returns!

How long, O Lord? I would batter down your gates with this great energy you have enfleshed! Do not leave me in desolation or false striving! Raise your Spirit within me and awaken our centerless union!

When such bold prayer fades from my lips, and I move through the day with merely spotty presence between the grasping and fearing, the one thin thread of sanity lies in patience.

Fool, all lies in a passion of patience, my lord's rule![63]

Simply Living

It is enough, my friend, to be where we are. You and I are given as much as we can bear for now. We will not be given more than that. Trust with me this patient truth, and the One

---

[63]C.S. Lewis, *That Hideous Strength* (Macmillan, 1965), p. 194.

who bears us through it. Then the simple way can live. Such a way someday will bear us Home, since:

God loves all simple things
For God is the simplest of all.[64]

[64]From the hymn, "A Simple Song", by Stephen Schwartz and Leonard Bernstein, in Leonard Bernstein's Mass (Columbia Records).

El Toro
Matline Ford

714-859-4942
25216 Rosewood